AF328783

SEX MACHINE

Charles Muller and Peggy Sastre

SEX MACHINE

Max Milo

Max Milo Éditions
Collection Mad Max Milo, Paris, 2023
www.maxmilo.com
ISBN : 978-2-31501-227-5

Prologue: Gene and Pleasure

You're reading this right now. By definition, your human ancestors all survived and reproduced until the happy event of your birth. And before them, your pre-human ancestors. We could trace your family tree back to the first single-celled life forms to populate the Earth. Our great-great-...-great-grandmothers are all microbial forms quite similar to some of today's bacteria.

In this long interval of hundreds of millions of years, life has produced some astonishing inventions. Sexuality is one of them.

Men and women today: sex machines?

One might think that the ancient biological mechanisms of sexual evolution have no effect on humanity today. This would be to overlook the obvious: while our bodies live in the unprecedented comfort of modern cities and open societies, our genes were also selected in the savannahs of the Pleistocene, when humans lived in small, closed groups.

In this book, you'll discover some fifty recent scientific studies that have explored the mysteries of our sexual behavior, particularly in the light of Darwinian evolutionary theory. You'll discover that the biological determinants of our evolutionary past have not disappeared, and still exert their influence, sometimes discreet, sometimes important, on the seemingly random interplay of our desire and pleasure.

So are we all "sex machines", unconscious vehicles of our Darwinian programming, willing slaves to the strategies of our genes? Only partly, because the development of the human brain has considerably widened the field of possibilities. But this slow evolution of free will has not erased our older determinations. Here's how they work in the sexual arena.

PART ONE

Men, Women: The Laws of Attraction

LET'S GET FEMININE!

Sexual dimorphism and facial attractiveness

The astronomical profits of cosmetics multinationals are based not only on the manipulation of the masses through marketing, but also on the empirical observation of several hundred million women: a well-made-up face is generally considered more desirable. And traditional societies untouched by globalized capitalism are no slouches when it comes to decorating the body and face - quite the contrary. To what extent are certain facial features considered more attractive than others? A team led by D. I. Perrett, a psychologist at the University of Saint Andrews (Scotland), has devised an original experiment to answer this question.

The researchers' starting point is the well-known relationship between hormones and facial features. In men, testosterone stimulates growth of the jawline, cheekbones, superciliary arches and nasal bridge. In women, estrogen has the opposite effect, but modifies other features such as lip size (the famous full lips). So there are more and less feminine and masculine faces. In

11

their experiment, Perrett's team used the miracles of computer morphing to vary these indices of virility or femininity on several portraits of individuals, some European, some Japanese. For each portrait, there was an initial untouched version and several versions, some feminized, some masculinized. A virtual plastic surgery operation in all its nuances, on 174 different points of the face. The photographs were of young students with no physical abnormalities, posing with a neutral expression under exactly the same studio lighting. Fifty subjects of European origin and 42 of Japanese origin, aged 18 to 44 - 48 men and 44 women - then rated each portrait on a continuous seduction scale.

For female faces, the extra "femininity" was appreciated by all participants, whatever their ethnic origin and that of the face being presented. The researchers noted a general preference for endogamy, i.e. European subjects were on average rated more highly by Europeans, just as Japanese were by Japanese. But in both cases, and also for inter-ethnic cross-judgments, feminized female faces won out over original and, a fortiori, virilized faces. The additional feminization rate varied from 10 to 22% depending on the face-spectator category. This feminization is associated with youth and fertility, known to be criteria of choice for men (and women, for that matter).

And what about men? The opposite effect is by no means true. On the contrary, men whose faces have been excessively masculinized are judged the least attractive, to the benefit of those whose features have been given a little feminine touch (a little less marked, however: 9 to 22% feminization). The beauty secret for both sexes seems to be the same: to look a little more feminine! In the case of men, the result may come as a surprise, since the dominance associated with masculine features is otherwise a valued trait. But excessive virility, and therefore dominance, can also be an indication of more negative traits such as coldness, violence and infidelity. This choice of slightly feminized men is compatible with the designation of kindness and empathy as important selection criteria for a long-term sexual partner. A father hen rather than a fickle husband, as it were.

D. I. Perrett's experience means you can now spend more informative moments in your dentist's or hairdresser's waiting room. As you watch the lives of your favorite "peoples" - Brad Pitt, Orlando Bloom, Georges Clooney, Johnny Depp, Monica Bellucci, Adriana Karambeu, Scarlett Johansson, Angelina Jolie and so on - think about noting the feminine or masculine features of their faces. After a certain number of observations, you'll be able to start making personal statistics. And perhaps better understand the secrets behind the worldwide popularity of these glamorous icons.

Reference

D. I. Perrett *et al* (1998), "Effects of sexual dimorphism on facial attractiveness", *Nature*, 394, 884-887.

LOVE, GLORY AND BEAUTY

Spousal choice and Darwinian logic

You've met your soul mate. You've had a fair or unfair wedding. You had beautiful children. And then you died, because all good things must come to an end. In the meantime, you've taken a rather important step: you've reproduced. Not you directly, in fact, but the half of your genes that ends up in your children.

David Buss, now a psychologist at the University of Texas, is a world-renowned specialist in Darwinian research on human sexuality. His 1989 article is one of the most cited in the literature on the subject. What's it all about? To find out whether the sexual preferences of today's humans, from a long-term union perspective, still conform to the predictions of Darwinian theory. David Buss sent the same questionnaire to 10,047 individuals worldwide, from 37 different cultures, six continents and five islands. Answers came from African hunter-gatherers to Western city-dwellers. They were all about the portrait of the "ideal partner".

First prediction: on average, women attach more importance to a good financial situation than men, as this guarantees a better potential for parental investment in their future children. This trait is found in 36 of the 37 cultures studied, even in those where female employment is widespread. Second prediction: men attach more importance to youth than women, as a guarantee of better fertility potential. This preference is found in all cultures, and is also borne out by the reality of unions (on average, men marry women younger than themselves in all societies). In fact, the survey shows that women themselves express a preference for partners slightly older than themselves. Third prediction: men attach more importance to beauty than women. The same result across all cultures: men were more likely than women to emphasize the physical attractiveness of their partner.

From a Darwinian point of view, the big question in life is: will an organism's genes be passed on to the next generation? This requires the individual to survive and reproduce, i.e. to produce viable offspring. In other words, natural selection (survival) and sexual selection (reproduction). In the context of sexual selection, evolutionary theory predicts that men and women do not value the same traits in their potential mates. This is due to the fundamental asymmetry of the two sexes: women have only one ovum, which is quite rare and produced once a month over a limited period of time; men have many spermatozoa, which are produced continuously, often throughout their lives. The genes of a male and female carrier therefore do not necessarily have the same strategies for reproducing from one generation to the next. On its own, a single man could impregnate a few million women: as many children would be born, which is a priori the aim of the species (to reproduce). But a single woman, faced with a few million men at her disposal, couldn't outrun the music.

As for the qualities of kindness and intelligence, they are also often cited as partner selection criteria. Which just goes to show the relativity of these studies, because if humans did what they said, wouldn't we have long since become a gentle, genial animal?

References

D. M. Buss (1989), "Sex differences in human mate preferences. Evolutionary hypotheses tested in 37 cultures", *Behavioral and Brain Sciences*, 12, 1-49.

D. M. Buss (1994), *The Evolution of Desire. Strategies of Human Mating*, New York, Basic Books.

THE RUSE OF THE SUBMISSIVE WOMAN

Male attractiveness and social hierarchy

The company boss having an affair with his secretary or accountant is a classic example of a para-professional relationship, a cliché of the corporate world as an extension of the realm of sexual struggle. But is men's attraction to their subordinates a simple abuse of power limited to one-night stands? Nothing is less certain.

Stephanie L. Brown and Brian P. Lewis (University of California, Los Angeles, National Institutes of Mental Health) looked at men's and women's preferences in relation to entrepreneurial hierarchies. They placed 328 volunteers (120 men, 208 women) in an imaginary work situation: they were shown photos of men (for the women) or women (for the men) presented either as assistants ("low dominance"), colleagues ("neutral dominance") or superiors ("high dominance"). Each time, the volunteers were asked to judge the photos on a scale of 1 to 9, according to three questions: can you imagine spending a night with this person, having an affair with this person, marrying this person?

Relationships of domination did not influence the judgment of women, who showed no particular correlation between sexual or marital attractiveness and hierarchical status. The same is not true of men: their choice is not random, and shows that on average they prefer a lasting affair or marriage with a subordinate woman. Our results show that men's preference for subordinate women increases when the investment required by the relationship also increases," emphasize the authors. This trend is consistent with the hypothesis of a reproductive advantage for men. Insofar as female infidelity is a severe reproductive threat only in cases where they invest heavily in their relationship, preferring a submissive partner may represent an advantage - which is not necessarily the case in a one-night stand."

Previous research has shown that women showing signs of vulnerability are, on average, considered more attractive by men. And this research ties in with a fairly well-established trend in most societies: on average, men prefer partners who are younger and have lower incomes than their own. The relationship of dependence thus created in these unequal couples therefore seems to flatter the (conscious or unconscious) desire for mastery in the male gender.

Sociologists such as Pierre Bourdieu have often considered male domination from the angle of symbolic and economic capital. The question should no doubt also be considered from the angle of biological capital. This capital is more difficult to modify, of course, as it has been accumulating for several million years...

Reference

S. L. Brown and B. P. Lewis (2004), "Relational dominance and mate-selection criteria. Evidence that males attend to female dominance", *Evolution and Human Behavior*, 25, 6, 406-415.

Marilyn Forever

Waist-to-hip ratio and physical attraction

What do the Venus de Milo, Marilyn Monroe and Claudia Schiffer have in common? Their *waist-to-hip* ratios, i.e. the value of waist circumference divided by hip circumference. The waist-to-hip ratios of these three models are 0.65, 0.61 and 0.67 respectively.

Devendra Singh came up with the idea of analyzing the role of waist-to-hip ratio in the physical attractiveness of women. A professor in Ohio's Department of Psychology, specializing in the links between physiological criteria and reproductive success, this researcher interviewed a thousand males aged 18 to 86, from different cultural and socio-economic backgrounds. The volunteers were asked to rate photographs of full-face women on a scale of physical attractiveness (sexual desire). The researcher's conclusion: the most desirable women are those with a waist-to-hip ratio between 0.6 and 0.8, with 0.7 as the median value. This conclusion was confirmed by two other analyses, one carried out on an all-student population, the other on the Miss

America of the last sixty years. Breast size was also found to be an important criterion (with an equivalent waist-to-hip ratio, larger breasts are preferred), but not decisive (apart from a good waist-to-hip ratio, breast shape and volume become irrelevant).

D. Singh's discovery gave rise to a flood of studies on the subject. All have confirmed the importance of the waist-to-hip ratio. Ronald Henss used a slightly different technique to verify this: he showed his guinea pigs retouched photos, with sometimes higher, sometimes lower waist-to-hip ratios for the same woman. Once again, the 0.7-0.8 range was the most popular, all other things being equal. The women included in this study proved to be more demanding than the men, with a ratio more often between 0.6 and 0.7.

Is this preference universal? More or less. Three researchers (Frank Marlowe, Coren Apicella and Dorian Reed) have analyzed the tastes of the Hadza people, a tribe of hunter-gatherers from Tanzania who, on the face of it, are not contaminated by the models, actresses and singers with dreamy bodies who populate the Western media. The preferred waist-to-hip ratio of our African hunters is 0.9 when assessed from the front. But when they're shown profile photos, showing the bounce of the buttocks, this ratio drops to 0.6, a lower value than in the West. The average of the two assessments is 0.78, not far from what we see everywhere else.

Let's move on to the explanations for this phenomenon. This value of 0.6-0.8 doesn't seem arbitrary, but what makes it so desirable to men? The first criterion seems to be youth. Over the course of a lifetime, the waist-to-hip ratio is optimal in pubescent girls and young women, especially those who have not yet had children. A second criterion is fertility. Several studies in the USA and the Netherlands have concluded that a fairly low waist-to-hip ratio is a good predictor of women's fertility (their ability to get pregnant quickly when they want to). This seems to be due to high estrogen and low testosterone levels, which are a guarantee of regular ovulation. A third criterion is health: the waist-to-hip ratio is a good indicator of overall fat distribution, and when it's low, it signals a lower risk of obesity, diabetes, cardiovascular pathologies and various cancers.

We have to assume that these criteria, obviously unknown to our ancestors, have been progressively integrated into the unconscious judgment of physical attractiveness through the interplay of natural and sexual selection. The famous image of Marilyn Monroe wishing President Kennedy a happy birthday in a dress revealing absolutely nothing of her superb curves has not ceased to make men dream...

References

D. Singh (1993), "Body shape and women's attractiveness. The critical role of the waist-to-hip ratio", *Human Nature*, 4, 297-321.

R. Henss (1995), "Waist-to-hip ratio and attractiveness. Replication and extension", *Personality and Individual Differences*, 19, 479-488.

F. Marlowe *et al.* (2005), "Men's preferences for women's profile waist-to-hip ratio in two societies", *Evolution and Human Behavior*, 26, 458-468.

Is Mr. Everyman a Lady-Killer?

Average, symmetry, attraction

"Strangeness is the necessary condiment of all beauty", said Baudelaire. A beautiful face is rare, and distinguished by this rarity. This is how the extraordinary differs from the ordinary. If these ideas sound familiar, forget them. It seems that we humans are ultimately very sensitive to average faces. Average... in the truest sense of the word.

Judith H. Langlois is currently Director of the Children's Research Laboratory at the University of Texas (Austin). In 1990, she co-published a landmark paper on the analysis of human desire, which at the time aroused a wave of skepticism. Taking advantage of advances in computer technology, J.H. Langlois came up with the idea of creating composite portraits based on the average of several portraits. Thus, 336 young men and 214 young women were photographed in the same neutral poses. From this set, 96 portraits were selected and divided into three subsets of 32 portraits. Then the morphing began: Langlois and his colleague blended the portraits (up to a maximum of 32) to produce increasingly "average" faces, i.e. blending the particular features of each initial portrait.

Then came the day of reckoning for these chimerical creatures. 300 participants were enlisted to give their opinion on the faces presented to them. They rated the faces from 1 to 5, i.e. from "very repulsive" to "very attractive". The verdict was clear: average faces won out over single faces, and the more average the faces (made up of 16 or 32 other faces), the greater their success. Male and female composite faces scored very similarly on average (2.51 vs. 2.43), indicating that both sexes benefit equally from the regression-to-mean process.

The uniqueness and rarity of beauty would not go down without a fight, even in the laboratory. Twenty or so similar experiments have been carried out since 1990, but all have come to the same conclusion: average faces are decidedly more pleasing than others, and this trend is statistically very robust. But it's not the only criterion: similar experiments have shown that the most symmetrical faces (created artificially by replicating half a face) are also those that elicit the strongest physical attraction on average. Nature's little imperfections, which are supposed to contribute to everyone's charm, have not withstood computer-assisted smoothing. In fact, some studies have even succeeded in reproducing the result with real faces, initially selected as the most common in their sample, then obtaining very high attractiveness scores (from another panel).

Not all medium-sized (or symmetrical) faces are attractive, but on average they are a little more attractive than others. Several explanations have been put forward. One is the correlation between regular facial features and good health, while strong asymmetries or deviations from the average are sometimes the sign of a developmental disorder. Another explanation, of a cognitive nature, suggests that our brain develops a bias to prefer what is familiar, known: we tend to appreciate standardized prototypes rather than limited series, so to speak. But there's no unanimity on the question yet. The research on average faces has the merit of answering a question we all asked ourselves in our youth: "No, but how does such a common guy (girl) manage to fall for such a gorgeous girl (guy)?" Perhaps truly common people aren't so common at all: they're more likely to be found in the computer morphs of laboratories than in everyday life.

References

J. H. Langlois and L. A. Roggman (1990), "Attractive faces are only average", *Psychological Science*, 1, 115-121.

G. Rhodes (2005), "The evolutionary psychology of facial beauty", *Annual Review of Psychology*, 57, 199-226.

Opposites Don't Attract

Genetic basis of assortative mating

In popular psychology, there are two main conceptions of lasting relationships between a man and a woman, referred to by the Anglo-Saxons as "romantic partners" (the affair of a lifetime) as opposed to "sexual partners" (the affair of a night). Some say we're attracted by our opposites, others by similarity. Science favors the latter.

As a general rule, sociological, psychological and biological studies conclude that spouses are similar in many respects: socio-economic background, level of education, race, IQ, personality, height, moral and political convictions. This is known as *assortative mating*. Some studies have shown that *assortative mating* involves more than just easily discernible physical or psychological traits. For example, an analysis of 1,000 couples of European origin showed a significant difference in the number of children depending on whether ten blood group markers of the spouses were close or far apart.

The question is, of course, whether this attraction to those who resemble us, in long-term unions, is the dominant fact of conditioning by our environment. Or is it a more innate tendency in human behavior? To find out, two psychologists from the University of Ontario (Canada), J. Philippe Rushton and T. Ann Bons, used a questionnaire containing 130 questions on a wide range of physical, psychological and socio-economic topics. The questionnaire was completed by 174 pairs of identical twins (monozygotic, 100% nuclear genes in common), 148 pairs of fraternal twins (dizygotic, 50% genes in common), 322 couples, 563 friends (defining themselves as best friends).

First result on the whole questionnaire: there's a positive correlation for all participants. This means that traits and attitudes tend to be similar for friends and lovers (siblings too, of course). A zero or negative correlation would have meant that participants have only a minority of points in common across the 130 traits studied. Second result: identical twins are the most alike (0.53 correlation), followed by fraternal twins (0.32). But spouses are just as similar (0.32), and best friends aren't far behind (0.22). This comes as a surprise, as it means that husband and wife have, on average, as many traits in common as siblings. Third result: similarity scores vary according to relationship and subject.

For spouses, the strongest correlation concerns work (0.74), followed by political ideas (0.60), level of education (0.55), income (0.43) and religion (0.41). Physical factors (height and weight) are positively correlated, but to a lesser extent (0.21 and 0.25), although they have a very strong genetic basis (heritability of 0.74 and 0.62). And certain psychological factors such as extraversion or neurosis are even less associated in husbands (0.06 and 0.01), again despite a strong genetic basis (estimated heritability of 0.90 and 0.66). On average, however, the search for similar traits in long-term partners (lovers and friends) is slightly stronger for the most heritable traits than for the least heritable. But a large proportion of elective affinities are not conditioned by genes.

Like attracts like: the proverbial wisdom wasn't entirely wrong when it came to friends and spouses. Over time, we tend to seek out the company of individuals who reflect our own traits and attitudes. Even if those who are most opposed to us are sometimes those who leave us with the best memories. What's more, it's not impossible that time spent with someone will eventually erase differences...

Reference

J. P. Rushton and T. A. Bons (2005), "Mate choice and friendship in twins. Evidence for genetic similarity", *Psychological Science*, 16, 7, 555-559.

Seeking a Man, Good Prospects

Environment and female partner selection

As we now know, the qualities preferred in partners with a view to a long-term union differ between the sexes. But we can also assume that other factors determine preferences. This is the case in the animal world, where population density and resource abundance influence pairings. Is this flexible mate selection true of the human species? Are we conditioned by our environment when looking for our soul mate?

To find out, Kevin J. McGraw, from the Department of Behavioral Neurobiology at Cornell University (USA), undertook a vast qualitative and quantitative study of matrimonial ads. His research focused on ads posted by women in the press: 23 different cities, 100 ads per city, a total of 2,300 messages from lonely hearts looking for a partner. In each city, K. McGraw analyzed the state of resources (average cost of living, average per capita income), the "sex ratio", women's participation in the workforce (ratio of working women). With regard to the actual content of the ads, the researcher distinguished four properties in the profile of the desired partner: emphasis on resources, physical qualities, emotional qualities or hobbies.

The criterion most widely and regularly highlighted is emotional qualities: in 22 out of 23 cities, it's on this point that the ads are most expressive. This result is not surprising: emotional stability is a guarantee of the longevity of romantic relationships and the quality of parental investment in children. Physical attractiveness comes second overall, but with greater variability between cities and in the degree of importance attached to this aspect. The same applies to resources and hobbies, which come next.

But a more detailed analysis of the correlations between environments (type of city) and ads (type of criterion) reveals other interesting phenomena. For example, population density correlates more strongly with resources (0.59) than with emotions (0.27), and this difference is even more marked for the cost of living, this time with a negative correlation with feelings (0.39 vs. - 0.48). The future spouse's resource availability is therefore valued in direct proportion to the importance of resources in the environment under consideration. In a world of rich people, we prefer to look for rich people. In a world of poor people, the income factor becomes more secondary.

Another point: in populated cities with a high female labor force, women put much less emphasis on personal interests and hobbies (- 0.79 and - 0.33), as well as emotions in the case of a high female labor force sex ratio (0.06). Physical attractiveness does not show highly differentiated correlations across environments: the only strong association is found with ads where women themselves highlight their physical qualities (0.55). This is a fairly classic illustration of assortative matching, with the choice of obvious and similar physical characteristics in the potential partner. Beautiful ladies - or those who consider themselves so - seek handsome gentlemen.

We know that to be attractive and happy, there's nothing like being young, handsome, rich and healthy. But when it comes to attracting certain women, the relative weight of these qualities changes according to their importance in the immediate environment. A repeated failure in the search for your ideal partner can therefore find an unexpected solution: moving.

Reference

K. J. McGraw (2002), "Environmental predictors of geographic variation in human mating preferences", *Ethology*, 108, 303-317.

SURVIVAL OF THE RAPISTS

The adaptability of rape in human evolution

When a man wants to sleep with a woman, seduction is one solution. Prostitution is another. But there's a third way, and unfortunately it's a very common one: rape. In France, reported rapes vary from 2,000 (in the 1990s) to 4,000 (in the 2000s) a year, but it is estimated that the number of reported rapes is still lower than the number of rapes committed but not reported. 99% of convicted rapists are men, and 96% of victims are women. The proportion is identical in all societies.

Biologist Randy Thornhill has been analyzing the issue of rape since the early 1980s. In 2000, he co-authored with C. T. Palmer an essay on the natural history of rape in the animal and human world, which provoked considerable controversy in the USA. Thornhill's hypothesis is that rape is not only a by-product of male aggression, but also an adaptive advantage for the rapist if he passes on his genes during forced intercourse. In other words, rape would have been frequent over the past hundreds of thousands of years, and its relative "success" compared to consensual procreation would have allowed this behavior to recur right up to the present day.

As is often the case in evolutionary theory applied to human affairs, the hypothesis is not easy to test. Nevertheless, Todd K. Shackelford, a psychologist at the University of Florida, has attempted to verify one of his predictions: if rape has an unconscious reproductive purpose, victims at the height of their fertile years must be over-represented. To obtain interpretable statistics, Shackelford compared female victims of rape-related murder and robbery-related murder in the USA between 1976 and 1994. In this case, murder by definition excludes the hypothesis of a conscious desire to reproduce. But the two situations allow us to see the profile of victims of comparable situations of violence (homicide), where the only difference is the concomitant act (rape or robbery). If rape simply expresses male aggression, it should follow a distribution comparable to that of theft in these precise cases.

Over the period analyzed, there were 564 homicides involving rape, and 1,289 homicides involving theft (of female victims, it should be remembered). In the first case (rape), the victim age probability curve (in relation to the overall population age group) peaks at 20-24, which is also the optimum age for female fertility. The curve then decreases steadily until the age of 74, but there is a second peak for women over 75. In the second case (theft), the age curve is very different, roughly stable from age 20 to 60, then rising to reach a distinctly high peak at age 75 and over. On the guilty side, young men are over-represented in both cases, with similar curves showing a peak at 20-24.

This work confirms on a large scale three previous studies on smaller databases. It's not enough, of course, to conclude definitively that rape arises from a residue of adaptive behavior during evolution - still less that "normal" human psychology is an unconscious desire to rape, as feminist statements have sometimes suggested. But it is yet another clue in the troubled genealogy of the human beast.

References

T. K. Shackelford (2002), "Are young women the special targets of rape-murderers?", *Aggressive Behavior*, 28, 224-232.

R. Thornhill and C. T. Palmer (2000), *A Natural History of Rape. Biological Bases of Sexual Coercion*, Cambridge (MA), MIT Press.

JEALOUS AND JEALOUSY

Evolution, jealousy, infidelity

Jealousy is a bad habit, they say. It's also a dangerous passion, ruining couples and even making a small contribution to crime statistics every year. The motivations behind jealousy are profound, since it can destroy the loved one. For evolutionary psychologists, accustomed to viewing humanity through Darwinian glasses, jealousy is the predictable result of sexual selection. Seducing a partner is one thing, keeping him or her is another, just as important: it presupposes that everyone is on guard against the forces that can dissolve the couple, foremost among which is the irruption of a tempting third party.

However, Darwinian logic readily speaks of jealousies in the plural. For each sex has different reasons for being afraid of its partner's infidelity, and therefore for being jealous. For men, the main threat is sexual infidelity, the direct result of which can be illegitimate offspring - that "child in the back" sharing no genes with its supposed father. Before paternity testing, in other words for 99% of human evolution, this outcome was impossible to verify, just as divorce was not an option. For the woman, the major risk is emotional infidelity, i.e. the possibility of her partner becoming so attached to a competitor that she leaves home altogether. Or, in more generic terms and more in keeping with our Paleolithic past, to minimize her marital and parental investment, essential to the survival of her offspring.

This would suggest that male jealousy is predominantly sexual, while female jealousy is predominantly emotional. To test this hypothesis, a team led by David M. Buss designed a questionnaire reflecting real-life scenes in which the two forms of jealousy are clearly distinct and the possible responses mutually exclusive. Administered to 1,122 North American subjects (374 men, 748 women), the test concluded that men are twice as anxious about sexual infidelity as they are about emotional infidelity. Another test was devised, in the form of a slightly more complex questionnaire in which six dilemmas were presented, mixing to varying degrees emotional and sexual jealousies (from the purest to the most mixed forms), as well as judgments about oneself or one's partner. This second questionnaire was administered to 234 Americans, 190 Koreans and 316 Japanese. The difference in perception between the sexes was found in these new studies. The subjects least sensitive to the distinction between emotional and sexual jealousy were the Japanese, indicating a certain cultural influence on the issue. We know that in Japan, the fact that a married man can have a few periods of recreational sex outside the household - sex without emotion, in other words - is more commonly accepted.

"Jealousy is a self-generating monster, born of its own womb", observed Shakespeare in *Othello*, the most accurate play on this painful and dangerous passion. French genius echoes this through Corneille: "Jealousy blinds a stricken heart / And, without examining, believes everything it fears." But men and women don't believe in the same fears.

Reference

D. M. Buss *et al.* (1999), "Jealousy and the nature of beliefs about infidelity. Tests of competing hypotheses about sex differences in the United States, Korea, and Japan", *Personal Relationships*, 6, 125-150.

SECOND PART

DESIRE, PLEASURE AND SEVENTH HEAVEN

Unequal in the Face of Desire

Genetics of individual sexual differences

It's a phenomenon we generally observe as early as school: some individuals seem more sensitive to sexual desire than others. Why should some be repressed and others liberated? We generally attribute these differences in behavior to upbringing, which is more or less open to these questions. Or to personality, with shy people and introverts finding it hard to express their desires properly. But what if this difference was already inscribed in our genes? This hypothesis was recently tested by Prof. Richard P. Ebstein's team. This specialist in molecular psychiatry heads the Scheinfeld Center for Human Genetics in the Department of Psychology at the Hebrew University of Jerusalem.

The researchers recruited 148 volunteers, 96 women aged 20 to 33 and 52 men aged 19 to 34. Subjects were asked to fill in a detailed questionnaire on their sexual behavior: importance of sex in their lives, frequency of arousal, existence of fantasies, difficulties during intercourse (vaginal lubrication, maintenance of erection). In order to minimize the bias of "over-representation of self", the questionnaire was anonymous, individual and completed via the Internet, so that volunteers had no particular reason to value themselves over others, whose answers they did not know. Once this stage had been completed, the researchers had a score for each individual on three points: desire, arousal, functioning (during the act).

The second step was to observe the genotypes of these patients. Richard Ebstein's team did not randomly target the tens of thousands of genes in our genome. A previous study on rats had shown that a gene coding for a dopamine receptor agonist (D4) is involved in erection and the frequency of acts in rodents. The homologue of this gene (DRD4) was therefore studied in our 148 human guinea pigs. Dopamine is a brain neurotransmitter, a chemical messenger that organizes the behavior of neurons, and by extension that of individuals. So-called dopaminergic neuronal networks are involved in a large number of traits and attitudes, including pleasure and reward seeking.

The result: small variants of the DRD4 gene do translate into variations in sexual behavior, in both men and women. Three major polymorphisms of the gene (i.e. three slightly different forms) vary desire, arousal and the quality of sexual intercourse. Variant D.4.4 is associated with low desire, while D.4.7 is at the top end of the scale. It seems that 30% of the population has a variant with high excitability, while 60% live under a more moderate regime. If the proportion were reversed, extramarital relationships would undoubtedly be much more widespread. According to previous work on the same gene

(Wang 2004), DRD4 mutations are of relatively recent origin, dating back 50,000 years to the time when modern humans migrated from Africa to colonize the world. The maintenance of different forms of the gene over the course of evolution would be associated with different behavioral strategies: less desire, more altruism and prosociality in one case; more desire, but also aggression and novelty-seeking in the other. Carriers of the "desire" variant would be the enfants terribles of our love and social relationships.

Of course, this work needs to be confirmed on larger, more diverse samples of the human species. If they are confirmed, they will have multiple consequences. Firstly, the DRD4 gene and its products could be the target of therapies aimed at correcting sexual dysfunctions, such as the hypoactive sexual desire disorder complained of by some women. We can also imagine the opposite scenario for those who suffer from permanent arousal, leading to family, professional or even legal problems. Secondly, as Richard Ebstein points out, "these advances in neuroscience allow us to take a new look at the variations in our sexual norms, without passing moral judgment". In this way, sexuality becomes a psychological and physiological activity like any other, de-dramatized, gradually escaping the age-old weight of social scrutiny and moral evaluation. Sex beyond good and evil, as it were.

References

I. Z. Ben Zion *et al.* (2006), "Polymorphisms in the dopamine D4 receptor gene (DRD4) contribute to individual differences in human sexual behavior: desire, arousal and sexual function", *Molecular Psychiatry*, 11, 8, 782-786.

E. Wang *et al.* (2004), "The genetic architecture of selection at the human dopamine receptor D4 (DRD4) gene locus", *American Journal of Human Genetics*, 74, 931-944.

BORN NOT TO ENJOY?

The genetic basis of frigidity

Is orgasm the most widely shared thing in the world? No. A study reveals that one in three women never - or rarely - experiences sexual pleasure. And this is true both during intercourse and masturbation: so there's no question of blaming the dictatorship of vaginal pleasure over clitoral pleasure, as the famous Hite report did in the 1970s. The most surprising fact is that this frigidity has a strong genetic component.

Kate Dunn works in the Genetic Epidemiology and Twin Research Unit at St Thomas' Hospital, London. She recruited around 4,000 women, including 683 pairs of monozygotic twins and 714 pairs of dizygotic twins. Each completed a self-questionnaire on orgasm. A third of the women questioned said they never felt pleasure. Comparing the answers of identical twins (who share 100% of their genes) with those of dizygotic twins (who share only 50%) and the rest of the population, Kate Dunn concluded that there is a genetic basis to this frigidity: around 34% of the differences between women in anorgasmia during the sexual act can be explained by genes, and this figure rises to 45% for clitoral anorgasmia.

As Kate Dunn points out, "our data suggest that differences in women's ability to have an orgasm have a biological basis, and therefore a possible evolutionary basis. Variations in this sexual function cannot be explained by cultural factors alone, although these also seem to play an important role." In the long term, the researcher hopes to identify the genes and proteins involved in this lack of sexual pleasure, firstly to better understand how it works, and secondly to develop treatments. This chemically-assisted enjoyment would enable all women to climb to seventh heaven, and some men to avoid the classic refusals due to migraines and other providential excuses.

The fact remains that this genetic anorgasmia represents an interesting enigma from an evolutionary point of view. For a gene to reproduce in a population, it is supposed to bring a selective advantage to its carrier. In the case of orgasm, this is easy enough to understand: it facilitates the formation of couples and their sexual fulfillment, thus increasing their probability of reproduction. But what can this adaptive advantage be in the case of the absence of orgasm? In fact, there are other hypotheses for female orgasm (Lloyd, 2005). It could be a by-product of the male orgasm: the clitoris and penis are formed from the same tissues during development, and selection would have acted primarily on penile pleasure, with females secondarily inheriting this capacity for sexual tissue excitability. In this case, the genes for anorgasmia are no longer a mystery, as female orgasm would not be the real target of selection and adaptation.

In any case, this difference between the sexes indicates that males and females are not always programmed to seek the same sexual gratifications. This has led to numerous conflicts throughout the history of couples, from the very beginning. In the last few hundred thousand years, a third of Homo sapiens females have learned to simulate pleasure to satisfy their partner's pride. Science is sometimes hopeless...

References

K. M. Dunn *et al* (2005), "Genetic influences on variation in female orgasmic function. A twin study", *Biology Letters*, Royal Society, DOI 10.1098/rsbl.2005.0308.

E. A. Lloyd (2005), *The Case of the Female Orgasm. Bias in the Science of Evolution*, Cambridge and London, Harvard University Press.

The Depressing Condom

The antidepressant effect of sperm

We've all experienced it: making love to the one you love is often an excellent mood tonic. And conversely, sexual solitude is rarely a good omen for joie de vivre. Beyond these generalities about the psychology of everyday life, researchers have taken a closer look at certain mechanisms that can change a woman's mood after sex. Surprise, surprise: sperm may possess some unsuspected virtues.

Gordon Gallup's team (New York University) recruited 293 heterosexual female volunteers. They completed a questionnaire specifying the frequency of sexual intercourse and condom use by their partner. In addition, the subjects' mood was measured by the Beck Depression Inventory, a standardized questionnaire. A score above 17 is interpreted as a sign of depression. The lower the score, the better the mood.

The result: women whose partners *never* use condoms scored 8, those who *sometimes* use condoms scored 10.5, those who *often use* condoms scored 15 and those who *always use condoms* scored 11.3. For women who don't have sex at all, the average score was 13.5. Another finding was that the longer the interval since the last unprotected intercourse, the more gloomy women's moods. This was not the case for women who had protected sex with a male condom. Finally, suicide attempts were also positively correlated with condom use.

This result was found on a larger sample (700 women), but this other study has not yet been published by Gordon Gallup's team. The anomaly in the score for women who *always* used condoms during intercourse (11.3, versus 15 for those who used them *often* and 10.5 *sometimes*) disappeared in this other study, showing that it was probably due to insufficient sampling.

The researchers' conclusion is simple: sperm has an antidepressant effect. All the other factors studied (frequency of intercourse, use of oral contraceptives, quality of the relationship, etc.) were not sufficient to eliminate the covariance of mood and the condom. There's nothing absurd about this hypothesis: male semen contains numerous hormones known to affect mood (prostaglandins, testosterone, estrogens, prolactin, etc.). And these molecules have been shown to peak in women's blood several hours after unprotected intercourse. Gordon Gallup is careful not to recommend abandoning the condom: "An unwanted pregnancy or STD largely annihilates the psychologically positive aspects of sperm", he points out. One of the paradoxes of this situation is that new-generation antidepressants often have the side-effect of reducing male libido.

Oral sex is supposed to have the same positive effects on mood, since the hormones are not destroyed by digestion. The same applies to the penetration of these molecules into the anorectal mucosa. The study does not say whether all sperm possess the same anti-depressant quality. You never know, the biggest donors might ask to be reimbursed by the French social security system, for services rendered to the mental health of the population...

Reference

G. G. Gallup *et al* (2002), "Sexual activity and depression. Does semen act as an anti-depressant?", *Archives of Sexual Behavior*, 31, 289-293.

Ejaculate to Fight Cancer

Ejaculatory frequency and prostate cancer

Is love good for your health? Beyond STDs, researchers are looking at the links between sexual behavior and health risks. The hypothesis that copulatory activity influences prostate carcinogenesis has long been dominant in the medical world. Since high ejaculatory frequency is indicative of high androgenic hormone activity, this would define populations at risk of hormone-dependent cancer. Another hypothesis is that sexual intercourse exposes subjects to cancer-causing pathogens, but such links have never been demonstrated in humans - unlike the link between uterine cancer and HPV exposure.

For Michael F. Leitzmann's team, the collection of epidemiological data confirming or refuting these various hypotheses was hitherto biased, being limited to interviews with men already suffering from prostate cancer. This researcher from the National Cancer Institute in Bethesda, Maryland, decided to broaden the sample. His study involved almost 30,000 males aged between 40 and 75, followed for eight years, from 1992 to 2000. The scientists asked them to estimate the number of times they ejaculated per month, including intercourse, nocturnal pollution and masturbation. This was done between the ages of 20 and 29, 40 and 49, as well as for the year preceding the start of the survey (1991), regardless of their age at the time. Participants could choose between several estimation groups: none, 1-3, 4-7, 8-12, 13-20, and over 21. At the end of the study, the results of the "none" and 1-3 categories were combined, due to the extreme rarity of responses mentioning no ejaculation.

The final analysis of the results was edifying: the men who ejaculated the most often were also those who suffered less frequently from prostate cancer at the end. Thus, the highest ejaculatory scores (an average of 21 times a month or more) were associated with the lowest tumor rates (a one-third reduction in risk). On average, an increase of three ejaculations leads to a 15% drop in cancer risk. From 12 ejaculations upwards, the benefits are clear, especially for cancers that progress slowly or are limited to the prostate. More aggressive cancers with rapid metastasis seem to be more indifferent to the sex life of their hosts. The researchers also noted that ejaculatory frequency was relatively stable across the lifespan, although the highest scores (more than three times a week) declined with age: 85% in their twenties versus 5% after the age of 60. We suspected as much. Finally, although these champions of ejaculation were more exposed than others to STDs, the researchers established no link between STDs and cancer pathologies.

This massive study confirms the findings of another study, this time carried out in Australia on 1,259 men. The team led by Graham Giles of Melbourne's Cancer Council Victoria had observed a correlation between masturbation frequency between the ages of 20 and 50 and a reduced risk of cancer. The figures were one-third lower for a masturbation frequency of five or more times a week.

Researchers are therefore developing new working hypotheses aimed at understanding why greater ejaculatory frequency reduces the risk of developing prostate cancer. Among these hypotheses, a better extraction of carcinogenic substances present in prostatic acini (groups of secretory cells forming at their center a canal where exocrine secretions are discharged) or a reduction in crystalloid microcalcifications often associated with cancers.

In any case: ejaculate, ejaculate, there will always be something left.

References

G. G. Giles *et al* (2003), "Sexual factors and prostate cancer", *BJU* (*British Journal of Urology*) *International*, 92, 3, 211-216.

M. F. Leitzmann *et al* (2004), "Ejaculation frequency and subsequent risk of prostate cancer", *Journal of the American Medical Association*, 291, 13, 1578-1586.

ORGASMATRON: BIONIC ECSTASY

Epidural implant treatment of anorgasmia

If we are to believe the magazines, those who complain about it or those who congratulate themselves on it, our modern times would consecrate the reign of enjoyment. No such luck for those who suffer from "orgasm disorders", the now medically correct term for the old "frigidity". Between 15% and 30% of the female population - a figure that varies according to polls and surveys - are said to be sexually disabled. And 65% will experience problems of this kind at least once in their lives. Good news for those who are affected and despair about it: a small device implanted in the spinal column could well stimulate orgasm and enable them to (re)experience sensations of sexual pleasure. This is what T. S. Meloy, an anesthesiologist and recognized pain management specialist.

In 2000, this researcher was working on substance-free pain reduction via electrical modulation of nerve flows in the spinal column. On a patient suffering from chronic low-back pain, he experimented with a percutaneous electrical implant in the epidural space, controlled directly by remote control. Once the device was switched on, the patient began to moan and writhe, and the monitors went wild: she was hyperventilating! The experiment is cut short, much to the despair of the volunteer, who then turns to Meloy and blurts out, "Now you must teach that to my husband!" The orgasmatron is born. Meloy decided to go one step further: put his orgasm pacemaker through clinical tests, prove that he could reproduce the experience, move from pain management specialist to sexual healer. And potentially win the jackpot.

FDA approval wasn't the hardest thing to get: Meloy had an oddly hard time finding volunteers. With a great deal of advertising, he finally managed to gather 11 volunteers aged between 32 and 60, all suffering from anorgasmia. This disorder is by far the most common in women. It involves a specific inhibition rather than a generalized disturbance of arousal, although the abnormality of arousal may be secondary to that of orgasm. As a general rule, the problem with anorgasmia is one of threshold: one is unable to reach a level of arousal such as to trigger orgasm. Meloy's patients suffered from primary anorgasmia (they had never experienced orgasm) for 6 of them, and secondary anorgasmia (the ability to reach orgasm had disappeared over time) for the other 5.

The device, the size of a small cigarette packet, consists of quadri- or octo-polar electrodes and is placed percutaneously directly on the spinal column. The eleven women were allowed to use the orgasmatron at home for nine days, interspersed with a visit to the laboratory at least every three days, and more often if necessary. They were also asked to keep a diary, recording the frequency of their sexual activities, the number of orgasms achieved and their strength (rated from 1 to 5). As an option, they could specify the quality of their vaginal lubrication, a known indicator of blood pressure and arousal. At the end of the nine days, 91% of patients felt a clear improvement in their sexual desire, and 40% (80% in secondary anorgasmics) reached orgasm with an average score of 3.25. One patient was excluded from the study, however, as she had not activated the electrodes once. Another was particularly enthusiastic: at the age of 48, she had not been able to orgasm for four years following menopause, and in nine days she reached orgasm seven times.

Quickly patented, the orgasmatron now awaits commercialization, at a price ranging from $13,000 to $17,000. After the mechanics of women, now it's time to connect them.

Reference

T. S. Meloy *et al* (2006), "Neurally augmented sexual function in human females. A preliminary investigation", *Neuromodulation*, 9, 1, 34-40.

THIRD PART

THE BRAIN IN LOVE

Everybody Obsessed?

Electroencephalography of ordinary eroticism

There's a widespread belief that men are far more sensitive to erotic images than women. In fact, over 90% of consumers of pornographic magazines and videos are men. Does this mean that women are indifferent to erotic material?

Andrey P. Anokhin is Assistant Professor of Psychiatry at Washington University School of Medicine in St. Louis, Missouri. He and his team recruited 264 female volunteers to watch a series of 55 slides. The slides depicted a variety of situations, including erotic and suggestive images of couples. Each slide remained on the screen for 6 seconds, with an obligation to look, and a pause of 12 to 18 seconds separating one visual from the next. As the ladies scrolled through the photos, an electroencephalograph (EEG) measured the electrical activity of their brains. The electrodes placed on their skulls specifically recorded what are known as "event-related evoked potentials" - small electrical discharges projected by neurons when they analyze an external stimulus.

Our neurons are very fast: they react even before we are aware of seeing an image. Yet - and the researchers admitted they were the first to be surprised - erotic images provoked a faster reaction than any other situation: 160 milliseconds, 20% better than the best scores recorded for other themes. Men always appreciate erotic images better," explains A. P. Anokhin. We therefore expected women to score less well on this kind of exercise." Not so.

The next step will be to use brain imaging to find out which areas are activated in this way, and whether they are the same in men and women. We already know that, in both sexes, certain areas of the prefrontal cortex work in concert with those of the visual cortex to differentiate categories. Is there an area of the brain specifically dedicated to the physical representation of love? Or does it more quickly trigger connections to older emotional areas of the brain?

What's certain at this stage is that our brains have been programmed by evolution to react particularly quickly to anything to do with sexuality. More detailed analyses may reveal slight inter-individual differences in this arousal of curiosity and desire. The secrets of our brains will thus be exposed. Will brain imaging one day become the post-religious form of the confessional?

Reference

A. P. Anokhin *et al* (2006), "Rapid discrimination of visual scene content in the human brain", *Brain Research*, DOI 10.1016/j.brainres.2006.03.108.

Romeo and Juliet Given a Scan

Crazy love and brain imaging

Love stories often end badly, but they always start well: love at first sight and the first few months after the declaration of reciprocal love are idyllic times, when lovers see life as rosy, are ready to lift mountains, and can't bear to spend a day away from the one they love... In short, an astonishing physiological and psychological transformation.

So what's going on inside these loving brains? To answer this question, all we have to do is look inside. An American team led by Arthur Aron, Debra Mashek and Greg Strong (New York University), with the help of anthropologist Helen Fisher (Rutgers University), used functional magnetic resonance imaging to observe the brains of 17 men and women madly in love. Each of these volunteers contemplated an image of the loved one, while the scanner penetrated the best-kept secrets of their neurons.

A number of characteristic features emerge in the bubbling brains of these Romeos and Juliets. Many regions are activated, but the dominant neural networks are those of motivation and reward-seeking: the dopaminergic system, in the ventral tegmental area, and the caudate nucleus near the basal ganglia. Some people with emotional attachment disorders (such as autism) have very little brain activity in this region. The brain regions involved in romantic love differ significantly from those involved in sexual desire. For example, the right hemisphere is clearly more activated than the left - the latter dominating when it comes to judging a partner's physical attractiveness, for example. "We wondered whether romantic love was simply superimposed on sexual desire. Our study answers that age-old question: love and sex do indeed differ from a cerebral point of view."

Just as interestingly, the neuronal physiology of love gradually changes over time. The brain undergoes changes as romance takes hold, notably with the activation of areas involved in fidelity: here we find the basal ganglia, sensitive to vasopressin, a hormone notably associated with attachment in social and sexual mammals. These data are very similar to those observed in other species, which may be experiencing the equivalent of our "love at first sight".

All these cerebral metamorphoses, common to all couples, show the important and ancient biological determination of our love relationships. These cerebral systems have probably evolved for important reasons," notes Helen Fisher, "for example, to concentrate the energy of seduction on certain individuals, and thus preserve it. Love at first sight may be a basic mechanism in some mammals, designed to speed up the pairing process."

In the not-too-distant future, lovers in crisis may be able to benefit from a new kind of couple therapy, where functional neuroimaging will pinpoint each partner's degree of attachment, fidelity and desire. And perhaps we'll be able to say: "I've scanned my soul mate.

Reference

A. Aron *et al*, (2005), "Reward, motivation, and emotion systems associated with early-stage intense romantic love", *Journal of Neurophysiology*, 94, 327-337.

Emotional Knockout

Orgasm and brain inactivity

It's well known that orgasm is a moment, always too short, when we disconnect from reality. This in itself is a strange phenomenon, as our brains are not used to this outside sleep phases. Instead, it has been programmed to remain vigilant. A team of Dutch researchers came up with the idea of using PET scans (positron emission tomography) to study the brain regions activated during orgasm. Their surprise was to find that, far from being explained by the activity of certain areas, the secret of orgasm lay in the inactivation of key regions, particularly those usually linked to emotions. What's more, this "emotional knockout" would be longer and more significant in women than in men.

The team led by Gert Holstege (University of Groningen) asked 13 healthy, heterosexual volunteers and their partners to come to their laboratory. After positioning their skulls under the scanner, the scientist gently asked them to engage in four types of sexual experience. The brain activity of each of these acts was then rigorously measured and compared with the others. First, the volunteers were asked to do nothing special. Then, they were asked to simulate. Then, their partner was called in to stimulate their clitoris. Finally, they were allowed to reach orgasm, again via clitoral stimulation.

The researchers thus discovered that, during sexual stimulation, areas of the primary somatosensory cortex are particularly activated, while others remain strangely silent, particularly in the amygdala and hippocampus, usually involved in situations such as vigilance or stress. Furthermore, analysis of the results indicates an orgasmic deficit in activity in areas of the prefrontal cortex, the seat of all higher cognitive faculties such as reasoning, anticipation or concentration. These areas were still active during simulation, but shut down completely during real sexual pleasure. For Gert Holstege, "these results show that, during orgasm, women have no emotional feelings. Everyone knows that fear and anxiety have to disappear to give way to pleasure, but we managed to see how this actually happened in the brain."

From an evolutionary point of view, this indicates that the brain "switches off" emotions during the sexual act, because the priority given to reproduction (justifying orgasm) manages to override that of individual survival (requiring vigilance). Holstege notes that extraordinary behaviours can be observed in other animal species, such as the hare becoming particularly reckless during the mating season. This urgency to find a sexual partner would then distance itself from caution in the face of predators, and find its fulfillment in orgasm. La Fontaine had it right: "Amour, amour, quand tu nous tiens, / On peut bien dire: Adieu prudence!"

One puzzle remains, however: why are so many regions inactivated during orgasm, when an extremely small number see their activity increase significantly, especially in the cerebellum? This area, involved in motor control and movement coordination, seems to be much more activated in women than in men, as shown by a previous study by the Dutch scientist. In the light of these two studies, he concluded that the female orgasm lasts longer than its male counterpart. The former can last up to two minutes, while the latter ends after just a few seconds. Whether intensity compensates for duration remains to be seen.

References

G. Holstege *et al* (2003), "Brain activation during human male ejaculation", *Journal of Neuroscience*, 23, 27, 9185-9193.
G. Holstege (2005), lecture given in Copenhagen at the 21st annual meeting of the European Society of Human Reproduction and Embryology (June).

Migraine and Other Bad Excuses

Migraine, serotonin, sexual desire

"Not tonight, darling, I've got a migraine". Everyone knows this popular cliché of the migraine excuse for declining a partner's sexual advances. It's usually attributed to women rejecting their partners. This could be justified by the fact that migraine affects women three times more than men. Or, more in keeping with the cliché, that men are reputed to be insatiable and women too quickly satiated. In any case, migraine and sexual activity are not supposed to go well together.

If the original work by Timothy Houle's team is to be believed, this image may soon disappear from our language. The researchers studied 68 volunteers of both sexes, with an average age of 24. All had suffered at least ten major headaches in the past year. The first task was to separate those with simple tension headaches (the most common type of headache, quickly resolved with aspirin or paracetamol) from those with true migraines (repeated headache attacks lasting several hours or even days, causing pulsations in the skull). Participants then completed a standardized questionnaire assessing their sexual desire, the Sexual Desire Inventory.

Study results: whatever their state of health, men reported more sexual desire than women (+24%). But men with migraines scored higher than men with headaches. And this difference was mirrored by women with migraines, whose scores exceeded those of their female counterparts, even equalling those of men with simple headaches. It should be noted that the questionnaire score corresponded to the participants' subjective assessment of their own level of desire in relation to the average. The researchers conclude that, provided this result is replicated on a larger sample, migraine seems to offer fertile ground for sexuality - between attacks, of course.

Is the result surprising? Not really. Several studies have shown that migraine attacks are partly associated with serotonin. This neurotransmitter, also implicated in depression, circulates in greater or lesser quantities in the brain. People with high serotonin levels suffer from sexual breakdown more often than others. And vice versa, for low levels. This systematic measurement study is the first of its kind, but an earlier study (Del Bene, 1982) of 362 migraine patients had already highlighted links with sexuality. Thus, 10% of these patients admitted to having flushes of sexual desire in the midst of an attack, and female migraine sufferers reported a greater number of fantasies than the average for their sex.

For the sake of completeness, we should also mention a rare condition known as sexual headache. Generally bilateral, it can be dull (pain intensifying with excitement or foreplay), explosive (intense pain during orgasm) or postural (pain occurring after coitus). The best prevention is to stop having sex. A real headache.

References

E. Del Bene *et al* (1982), "Sexuality and headache", *Advances in Neurology*, 33, 209-214.

T. T. Houle *et al.* (2006), "Not tonight, I have a headache?", *Headache: the Journal of Head and Face Pain*, 46, 6, 983-990.

DICKHEADS

Sexual desire and discounting the future

Don't let the title fool you: this is one of the most complex chapters in the book. Depending on what you understand, you'll know which category of knot you belong to: the impatient acorn or the trunk-solid foresighted one.

In popular parlance, a "knucklehead" means an "idiot". The knot in question is none other than the imaginary version of the penis, likened with a certain typically masculine pride to the hard knots in a tree trunk. Slang has also preserved the word "gland" as a synonym for both the male sex and stupidity personified (being an acorn). Is a dickhead a male who thinks with his sex rather than his brain? A recent experiment suggests so.

Margo Wilson and Martin Daly are both psychologists at McMaster University (Ontario, Canada), and have written some classic works on the evolution of human sexual behavior (see Wilson and Daly, 1982). In this study, 96 men and 113 women, with an average age of 19 and a half, were asked to start by looking at photographs of faces and cars. The volunteers were divided into four groups: those looking at beautiful faces, ugly faces; those looking at attractive cars, neutral cars. Just before and just after viewing the photographs, the volunteers played a computer game with a reward. But this game had a special feature: it gave them the choice between an immediate payout ($15 to $35 the next day) and a higher deferred payout ($50 to $75 within a year).

It's actually a game developed to analyze consumer behavior, more precisely what economists call "hyperbolic discounting of the future": in everyday life, individuals express impatience in the short term (high immediate discount rate), but a certain patience in the long term (low future discount rate). Hence the hyperbolic, rather than exponential, shape of the curve illustrating these preferences.

If this quick tour of economic theory has left you stumped, don't worry. Just remember that our preferences vary according to the time scale, and that we tend to value short-term profit. What does this have to do with faces, cars and sexuality in general? Daly and Wilson's experiment showed that only one category exhibited characteristic behavior during the game: men who had seen photographs of attractive women. These men have a clear tendency to value immediate gains over long-term ones. The others (men viewing ugly women or cars, women viewing men or cars, whatever their attractiveness) do not vary in their behavior. It should be added that women viewing portraits of good-looking men showed a similar trend, but of very low amplitude, bordering on significance.

How can we explain this specific attitude of young men confronted with desirable young women? We need to distinguish between distal (evolutionary) and proximal (neuropsychological) causes. From an evolutionary point of view, we know that males tend to favor short-term reproductive strategies: we can expect this to prompt them to also prefer short-term gains (a pronounced hyperbolic discount) enabling them to maximize this strategy. From a neuropsychological point of view, the neural circuits of sexual desire also activate the reward-enhancing circuits of the nucleus accumbens in the brain. The latter is connected to areas of the orbitofrontal cortex known to be involved in the search for monetary gain. The phenomenon is more pronounced in male than in female brains. Without the subject being aware of it, his slight arousal would push him towards a logic of immediate profit.

Daly and Wilson conclude their work with a suggestion for further reflection. In fact, hyperbolic discounting of the future is highly context-dependent, and provides us with information about certain social behaviors. The search for short-term gain at the expense of the long term is, for example, more pronounced in young people (who are therefore sensitive to ephemeral stimuli), but also characterizes social categories such as the poor (who are often in a situation where there is little to look forward to in the future) and judicial categories such as sex offenders. The way in which individuals perceive the opportunities in their environment therefore partly determines their "strategy" for adapting to available resources. And this by virtue of an evolutionary logic much older than the current framework of our societies.

To conclude on the initial theme of this reflection, men may not all be dickheads. But they do often behave like dickheads.

References

M. Wilson and M. Daly (1982), *Sex, Evolution and Behavior*, Belmont, Brooks Cole.

M. Wilson and M. Daly (2004), "Do pretty women inspire men to discount the future?", *Proceedings of the Royal Society of London*, Biological Sciences, 271, S177-S179.

I Should've been an Artist

Creativity, schizophrenia and sexual success

Discovered by Eugen Bleuler in 1911, schizophrenia is a strange and terrible disease of the mind. It leads to hallucinations, personality splits, inner voices, social marginalization and suicide. Schizophrenia is clearly hereditary, affecting around 1% of the adult population. This poses a bit of an evolutionary enigma: how could an illness as incapacitating as it is heritable be passed on from generation to generation, instead of disappearing? To solve this psychiatric mystery, Daniel Nettle (Newcastle University) and Helen Clegg (Open University) have formulated an interesting hypothesis: the tendency towards schizophrenia is greater in creative individuals, and this creativity is associated with a more intense sex life.

The underpinning of schizophrenia is a set of behavioral and personality traits known as "schizotypy". Several studies have shown that artists and creative individuals often score well on schizotypy questionnaires. Without being schizophrenic in the clinical sense of the term, creative people are said to possess a few "mental disorder" genes that give them their creative capacity. If, on the other hand, these same creative personalities are slightly more successful sexually than others, this could explain why certain genes involved in schizophrenia continue to spread through the population, despite the burden the disease represents when fully expressed.

Nettle and Clegg gathered 425 British subjects, with an average age of 40.5, divided into 156 men and 269 women. These volunteers were asked to complete a schizotypy questionnaire, assessing two personality traits in particular: the search for unusual experiences and non-conformist impulses. They also told the investigators about their lifestyle and, above all, the number of sexual partners they had had since the age of 18 (including very short relationships). Finally, they were asked to specify whether they were involved in poetry or art. Since recruitment had been partially oriented towards these milieus, 184 participants of both sexes found themselves in the artist category, compared with 241 with no creative activity.

Result: the two psychologists did indeed find a significant positive correlation between schizotypy, creativity and sexual success, indicating that the number of partners is not established at random when taking into account a population's artistic abilities. The more involved a person is in artistic tasks, the higher their scores on the sexual success scale (4.3 for non-artists, 4.3 for artists who are not very involved in their art, 5.4 for those who are fairly involved, 5.5 for those who are very involved). The search for unusual experiences was positively correlated with artistic activity (0.28), as were non-conformist impulses (0.05). These two schizotypal personality traits are also directly correlated with sexual success (0.09 and 0.19), whether or not they concern artists. And creativity itself also shows a positive correlation of 0.15 with the number of sexual partners. The correlations are weak, but significant nonetheless. While men have slightly more partners on average than women, both sexes benefit equally from creativity from a sexual point of view compared to the rest of the population.

This study confirms an interesting hypothesis put forward a few years ago by Geoffrey Miller: a large proportion of our artistic production, perfectly useless from the point of view of energy resources, would have developed over the course of evolution with the sole aim of seducing partners of the opposite sex. The first humans would have learned to sing, dance, decorate their bodies and paint, in order to seduce by displaying their quality, just as the peacock or the guppy display shimmering colors (and ultimately costly, even dangerous for their wearer, which indicates their quality to bear this cost). Now you know why the celebrity press is full of the sexual antics of the celebrities of the moment, who are always off to semi-mundane parties, going from break-up to reunion week after week. These artists and creative personalities, carriers of a few mental disorder genes, may just be expressing the excellent sexual performance with which evolution has endowed them. Three million years of hominization to get to Madonna, that's something to ponder.

References

D. Nettle and H. Clegg (2005), "Schizotypy, creativity and mating success in humans", *Proceedings of the Royal*

Society of London, Biological Sciences, DOI 10.1098/rsph.2005.3349.

G. Miller (2000), *The Eating Mind. How Sexual Choice Shaped the Evolution of Human Nature*, London, Heineman.

PART FOUR

Hormones, Pheromones and other Odors

The Taste of Others (and Your Own)

Scent recognition and incest avoidance

For those who wish to do so, i.e. almost everyone, avoiding incest seems obvious today. But let's immerse ourselves in a Paleolithic tribe of a few hundred or a few thousand members: no civil status, probable polygamy, deception there as elsewhere, swarms of children and teenagers of unknown parentage. And all this coexists at an age when television doesn't exist, so sexual activity is probably a more common pastime on long winter evenings or hot summer nights. Perhaps our ancestors already had rules prohibiting incest? But according to a highly original experiment led by Glenn E. Weisfeld (Wayne University, USA), they may also have guided their choices by more instinctive processes...

Three experiments were conducted by Weisfeld's team. In each case, the researchers examined whether the volunteers' responses differed from mere chance. Each of these tests pitted T-shirts worn by relatives or strangers against each other, and participants' ability to discriminate between odors alone. Those who wore the T-shirt for two consecutive nights were asked not to use any scented substances, and not to smoke during the period of impregnation.

First experiment: 22 adults (11 men and 11 women), aged between 19 and 46, had to recognize seven different smells: mother, father, brother, sister, unrelated relative, stranger. The experiment was repeated five times in succession, with the option of giving different answers if they thought they'd got it wrong beforehand. An answer was correct if the person gave the right attribution at least 3 times out of 5. Result: strangers were recognized in 91% of cases, mothers in 86%, relatives in 73%, brothers, sisters and fathers in 59%, oneself in 50%. Male odors were judged to be more intense than female ones, but this had no effect on the result. Conclusions: the stranger/relative distinction largely prevails, and the mother is always the best recognized among relatives.

Second experiment: 35 boys and 42 girls aged 4 to 11 were asked to wear the same T-shirt three nights in a row, and 18 mothers were asked to distinguish the smells of their children (37 of the 77) from those of the others. A small complication: of the 37 children, 7 were from a different diaper, and therefore not biologically related to their mothers. In addition, the children themselves had to recognize the scent of their siblings. Here, too, there was a slight complication: of all the children, there were 10 pairs of half-siblings, and 11 pairs where the other child was adopted (with no link to the biological mother or father). Result: the mothers recognized their biological children in 27 out of 30 cases. On the other hand, they recognized their adopted son in only 2 cases out of 7. The same trend applies to children: they were more likely to recognize their biological siblings (21 correct answers, 9 errors), slightly less likely to recognize their biological half-siblings (16 vs. 12), and even less likely to recognize their adopted siblings (10 vs. 18). Compared with random responses, only recognition of biological relatives was positive and significant. Conclusion: body odor recognition is associated with genetic proximity between individuals.

Third experiment: 21 families are involved this time, 17 with two children, 3 with three children, 1 with four children. The children range in age from 6 to 15, and the T-shirt procedure is applied to everyone. This time, not only did they have to recognize their father or mother (for the children) or their children (for the parents), but they also had to say in a prior experiment which smell they preferred between a parent's T-shirt and a non-relative's T-shirt (of course, only the examiner knew that a relative was involved; the participant simply had to say his or her choice between two apparently identical T-shirts). Results: both mothers and fathers recognized their children quite well (50 vs. 7 for mothers, 31 vs. 11 for fathers), but both preferred the smell of a stranger to that of their child (9 vs. 47, 15 vs. 27). Only children aged 9-15 (not 6-8) preferred to recognize their parents, both mother and father (18 vs. 5 for the mother, 32 vs. 6 for the father). Children reacted in the same way: they preferred the odors of strangers to those of their parents in the control test, just as they preferred the odors of strangers to those of their brothers or sisters of the opposite sex (13 vs. 27), but not especially of the same sex (22 vs. 26). This is an interesting result, since the risk of incest concerns children of the opposite sex.

What can we conclude from this game of seven scented families? Firstly, that related individuals recognize each other by their body odors, whether parent-child or sibling, and distinguish strangers from close relatives. Secondly, this recognition tends to be associated with aversion, i.e. foreign odors are preferred to those of close relatives. In short, it's as if we were unconsciously programmed to avoid incest and to use the most basic resource for recognizing others: their scent.

Reference

G. E. Weisfeld *et al* (2003), "Possible olfaction-based mechanisms in human kin recognition and inbreeding avoidance", *Journal of Experimental Child Psychology*, 85, 3, 279-295.

SMELL ORGAN OR NOT?

Human sensitivity to pheromones

Our conscious experiences account for only around 10% of mental activity. The brain is constantly interpreting signals from the internal or external environment without warning us. Could it be that our behavior is largely modulated by unconscious processes, such as sensitivity to chemical messengers?

Just over forty years ago, Karlson and Luscher coined the term "pheromone": a chemical message emitted by one animal that provokes a physiological or behavioral response in another animal of the same species. There are five types of pheromone: sex, gregarious, spacing, alarm and marking. Pheromones are classified into two groups: "releaser", when they induce rapid change, and "primer", when their influence on the neuroendocrine system is more diffuse and continuous. Mammals detect pheromones via specific receptors located in the vomeronasal organ (VNO). This small tubular structure is located in the nasal cavity of mammals. The pheromonal information deciphered by the VNO is then transmitted to the secondary olfactory bulb and other brain regions, such as the anterior zone of the hypothalamus. This area controls neuroendocrine systems, partly responsible for certain aspects of reproductive physiology and behavior. The VNO-brain circuit constitutes the secondary olfactory system, distinguished from the primary system, whose receptors are found in the epithelial cells of the nose.

A WNV has been identified near the base of the nasal septum in adult humans. It has long been considered an atrophied organ, a useless relic of its evolutionary history. Is it really non-functional? Humans, like all animals, emit odors from various parts of their body. An individual's specific odor is formed by various secretions, particularly those from the armpits (axillary zone). The biochemical composition of these secretions depends on several parameters: genetic, hormonal, metabolic, dietary, psychological and environmental influences.

Martha McClintock pioneered the study of the influence of pheromones on men. Nearly 25 years ago, she showed that the ovarian cycles of a group of women (roommates, close friends, convent nuns, etc.) tended to follow each other. In one famous experiment, cotton pads soaked in female body odor were rubbed under the noses of women who were asked not to wash their faces for six hours. This procedure was repeated daily for the duration of two ovarian cycles. The participants' biological clocks were then systematically affected. More specifically, scents collected from the axillary zone of women in the follicular phase of ovulation shortened the recipients' menstrual cycles. Scents taken from women in the midst of ovulation, or two days after ovulation, had the opposite effect on the recipients' cycles.

While the influence of pheromones on humans is no longer in doubt, an integrated understanding of the phenomenon, from gene to behavior, is still a long way off. In September 2000, a team of researchers at New York's Rockefeller University identified the first human vomeronasal gene, V1RL1, sharing 28% of its sequence with its rat and mouse counterparts. Seven of these sequences proved inoperative. An eighth produces a protein comparable to that used for pheromone recognition in rodents. This gene has subsequently been shown to undergo positive selection in primates.

"Human behavior is obviously much more motivated by sight than by smell," explains Yvan Rodriguez, co-author of the V1RL1 study. "We shouldn't expect that human pheromones, sold in 100 ml bottles, will enable some people to attract those they desire. This works very well in some animals, insects and rodents in particular, but we use a lot of additional information when we make a choice of partner." A bottle half-full: if pheromones don't explain everything, they do explain part of it... Commercial exploitation, however, was not long in coming. Senomyx, a Californian biotech company, intends to apply the latest scientific discoveries on the influence of scent on our behavior. Its scientific team includes Peter Mombaerts, co-discoverer of the V1RL1 gene...

References

P. Karlson and M. Luscher, (1959), "Pheromones. A new term for a class of biologically active substances", *Nature*, 183, 55-56.

L. Monti-Bloch *et al* (1998), "The human vomeronasal system. A review", *Annals of the New York Academy of Sciences*, 855, 373-389.

M. K. McClintock (1984), "Estrous synchrony: modulation of ovarian cycle length by female pheromones", *Physiology and Behavior*, 32, 5, 701-705.

N. I. Mundy and S. Cook (2003), "Positive selection during the diversification of class I vomeronasal receptor-like (V1RL) genes, putative pheromone receptor genes, in human and primate evolution", *Molecular Biology and Evolution*, 20, 11, 1805-1810.

K. Stern and M. K. McClintock (1998), "Regulation of ovulation by human pheromones", *Nature*, 392, 6672, 177-179.

I. Rodriguez *et al* (2000), "A putative pheromone receptor gene expressed in human olfactory mucosa", *Nature Genetics*, 26, 1, 18-19.

Happy Armpit

Pheromones, mood and luteinizing hormone

In our pornographic depiction of sexuality, we're all too happy with full body hair removal and compulsory hygiene. Yet body odor is a classic element of traditional eroticism. Could there be some obscure elixir of desire in the now odoriferously incorrect zones of our bodies?

Researchers at the University of Pennsylvania, led by George Preti, collected male armpit fumes on absorbent cotton. They then selected 18 women, aged between 21 and 45, heterosexual, without hormonal contraception, with regular cycles, practising a sporting activity. These women had no history of hirsutism, sleep disorders, thyroid disorders or galactorrhea. Their weight was within the normal range, plus or minus 15%.

The study took place over three complete menstrual cycles, defined as the stages of the experiment: basal, test and final cycles. During the first cycle, participants provided their basal body temperature and a morning urine sample to measure LH levels (luteinizing hormone, responsible, among other things, for ovulation in women). The same data were recorded during the second cycle, except that during the first week, volunteers had to have a cotton pad soaked in either 0.5 ml ethanol (placebo) or male axillary extract applied under their nose for twelve hours, with a refill every two hours. Blood samples were taken every ten minutes. The women were divided into two groups: one receiving placebo for the first six hours, and male axillary extract for the second six hours; the second group received placebo for the second six hours, and male axillary extract for the third six hours. To monitor any changes in the hormonal cycle induced by this experiment, measurements from the first cycle were repeated during the final cycle. A final note: neither the volunteers nor the nurses taking part in the operation were aware of the purpose of the study.

In addition to these collective inhalations of male armpit or placebo, the women were asked to rate their mood on a scale from 1 to 7, as well as to specify and quantify several states of mind: tense, tired, sexy or anxious. A questionnaire presented to the volunteers at the end of the study showed that none of them guessed the nature of the extract applied to their upper lip, with answers ranging from alcohol to perfume to lemony household product. Perhaps they thought they were dealing with one of those qualitative evaluation sessions that commercial brands are now so fond of.

The result: armpit scent had no influence on cycle length. However, women lucky enough to smell their male counterparts' axillary extracts experienced an improvement in mood and a significant drop in blood LH levels. For Charles Wysocki, "this discovery opens the door to important pharmacological innovations in ovulation modulation, treatment of premenstrual syndrome and natural anxiolytics. With a better understanding of how pheromone neuroendocrine responses work and their impact on mood, we can now imagine the creation of the perfect male scent."

Tomorrow, a real man may be recognized by a good level of hormones and a good level of mood. The former is undoubtedly more quantifiable than the latter.

Reference

G. Preti *et al* (2003), "Male axillary extracts contain phero-mones that affect pulsatile secretion of luteinizing hormone and mood in women recipients", *Biology of Reproduction*, 68, 6, 2107-2113.

The Contract of Trust

Oxytocin, confidence and seduction

Before sex, there's often a question of trust. At least in human beings, who are less inclined to the mechanical copulations during the ovulatory phase of their mammalian cousins. And beyond sex, trust can be found in friendship, family relationships and life in general. Without it, economic, social and political institutions would be likely to descend into chaos and war. But what exactly is the biological basis of this trust?

To answer this question, Michael Kosfeld's team (University of Zurich) devised a game simulating a situation where an investor gives his money to a trustworthy person who must invest it, without the investor receiving any guarantee of a return on his investment. The scientists discovered that investors were far more willing to give their money if they had been given an oxytocin spray to sniff beforehand. This effect disappears when the game is played on a computer - proof that oxytocin influences interpersonal relationships, not the individual's reckless risk-taking.

Produced by the hypothalamus and acting on the amygdala, two ancient regions of our limbic brain, oxytocin is one of the hormones circulating in the neuronal regions of emotion and sociality. It is commonly used in medicine to induce labor during childbirth and to facilitate milk production.

The fact that humans are sensitive to oxytocin opens up interesting avenues of research. Animal studies have already shown that this hormone greatly enhances approach and contact. In a series of experiments designed to understand the brain mechanisms at work in the choice of sexual partner, Donald W. Pfaff's team (Rockefeller University, New York) subjected female mice to two types of odors: one from males alone, the other from males accompanied by females. The females systematically preferred the second type of odor. In some cases, a male-female odor seasoned with a strong parasite odor was even preferred to that of a healthy male alone. When the oxytocin production gene was switched off in female mice, they no longer chose the odors of males with females, and were in fact unable to recognize those of a parasite-infested male alone, even though the integrity of their olfactory system (excluding oxytocin) was monitored.

For Pfaff, oxytocin is therefore directly involved in the production and integration of social information used by female mice to select their partners. Sexual choice is largely a copy of the sexual choice of others, based on olfactory cues. Females tend to trust the choices of other mice. While this "copying" is well documented in fish and birds, this is the first time its mechanism has been demonstrated in mammals.

A neurotransmitter of trust and attraction, oxytocin also seems to be active in men, as Kosfeld's study shows. We can already imagine many possible applications: oxytocin-enhanced perfumes to break the ice in nightclubs; oxytocin-enhanced election campaigns to break the mistrust of the scalded voter; oxytocin-enhanced stores to break the piggy bank of the captivated consumer. The contract of trust reviewed and corrected in the age of olfactory neurobiology.

References

M. Kosfeld *et al* (2005), "Oxytocin increases trust in humans", *Nature*, 435, 673-676.

E. Choleris *et al* (2006), "Involvement of estrogen receptor alpha, beta and oxytocin in social discrimination. A detailed behavioral analysis with knockout female mice", *Genes, Brain and Behavior*, 5, 7, 528-539.

THE SEXY SMELL OF MOMS

Breastfeeding and sexual desire

When a woman gives birth, family and friends flock to the maternity ward to rejoice at the happy event. But what if the company of a mother and her infant gave women a furious desire to reproduce?

This is the conclusion reached by Martha McClintock and Julie Mennella's team. In 2001, the latter had already demonstrated that exposure to the odors of breastfeeding women could modify the menstrual cycle of other women: those with long cycles had them lengthened, those with short cycles had them shortened. Four years later, a new experiment involving 26 breastfeeding women (8 of African origin, 18 of Caucasian origin) took the question further. Samples of their milk (with the baby's smell mixed in) and axillary perspiration were collected on cotton pads. These women had to exclusively breastfeed their children (13 girls and 13 boys aged 3 months "maximum), and had not yet regained their menstrual periods. They also had to follow a "neutral" diet to avoid contaminating the samples with spicy odours, and keep strict records of all solid and liquid intake during the test period. In the end, all participants scrupulously followed these dietary instructions. The final requirement was to wash with unscented hygiene products and wear a cotton pad in their bras for around eight hours every day. The cottons were then impregnated with neutral solutions to homogenize their color and texture, and frozen at -80°C.

47 nulliparous women were recruited from diverse backgrounds (62% Caucasian, 10% African, 2% Hispanic, 25% other ethnicities). The age range was between 18 and 35. All reported having regular cycles, being non-smokers and not using hormonal contraception. The absence of pregnancy during the three months required for the study was regularly monitored. The scientists asked them not to wear any perfume and did not inform them of the purpose of the study. At no point was the term "pheromone" mentioned. After smelling the cottons, they were asked to define the origin of these odors from a list of thirty entries, including "child odor", "perspiration" or "no odor". They were then asked six questions: Did you smell anything? If so, please specify (open-ended question)? How strong is the smell? Did you like the smell? Did you hate the smell? Do you think the smell affected your mood? In each case, a quantitative scale from 1 to 4 was proposed. More detailed questionnaires on mood and sexual arousal were also distributed, and hormonal measurements were taken.

Compared with the control group, women who smelled cotton soaked with the secretions of breastfeeding women saw their mood and arousal improve. In particular, they experienced a boom in the frequency and length of sexual intercourse, and in the number of sexual fantasies and thoughts in their daily lives. The scent of moms and their babies is therefore an incentive to motherhood, including of course sexuality, an essential prerequisite until cloning and artificial insemination become commonplace.

For the researchers, such responses to the chemical signals of motherhood were selected over the course of mammalian evolution, as they were undoubtedly clues to an environment conducive to reproduction and survival. The more viable babies there are, the more resources - and incentive pheromones - are available. Julie Mennella also notes that in many cultures, young mothers are encouraged to socialize with childless women, whereas parturients are often isolated during pregnancy. This may also explain the "fashion" phenomenon we often see around us, when sisters or friends follow in close succession during pregnancy.

Reference

N. A. Spencer *et al.* (2004), "Social chemosignals from breastfeeding women increase sexual motivation", *Hormones and Behavior*, 46, 3, 362-370.

THE SCENT OF LIBIDO

Synthetic pheromones

In a laboratory with white corridors on the outskirts of San Francisco, a singular experiment begins in the early 2000s. Thirty-six women aged between 19 and 48 are asked to freely alternate a mysterious substance with their usual perfume. The women were heterosexual and in good health. Some of the women leave with a placebo, while all are asked to detail their sex lives before and after the introduction of the fragrance: kissing, heavy touching, intercourse and masturbation, all the while keeping precise notes on the use of the perfume. The experiment lasts six weeks, the test period two. All participants believed they were testing new perfumes with evocative names such as Lolita, Bondgirl, Barbie Doll, or others with neutral names such as 41799 or AB123YZ. The substance's real code name, as far as the researchers are concerned, is Athena Pheromone 10:13. It's a synthetic compound of female pheromones extracted from various bodily secretions.

On average, the volunteers were not clearly more attracted to 10:13 than to the placebo, since the placebo group used the perfume 5.3 times a week versus 5.4 for the pheromone group. What did change, however, was the frequency and nature of sexual activity: 74% of the 10:13 group saw their sexual activity at least triple compared to the test period, particularly with regard to penetrative sex acts. The scientists also noted an increase in "spontaneous" rendezvous and intimate sessions, i.e. with complete strangers. In the placebo group, only 23% of participants saw their sexual activity increase in this way. In both groups, masturbatory activity remained comparable.

For Norma McCoy, who led the experiment, this is proof that these synthetic pheromones, already patented and whose precise composition is still kept secret, increase women's degree of attraction to men. The fact that masturbation does not seem to be affected suggests that women are not more aroused, but that men are more attracted. George Preti, who conducted a study with McCoy on the pheromones in sweat (see "Happy armpit" *above*), isn't convinced, however, that his colleague has properly purified the extracts they've been working on together since the 1980s, and cautions: "You have to be careful with dosages - if you use an extract that's too concentrated, you may not be happy with the result you get." Obviously, if all the males in the neighborhood fall on you when you wear 10:13, the result may not be pleasant. And likewise if an excess of the pheromone fragrance provokes a reverse reaction of flight from a potential partner deemed far too... voracious.

Reference

N. L. McCoy and L. Pitino (2002), "Pheromonal influences on sociosexual behavior in young women", *Physiology and Behavior*, 75, 3, 367-375.

Just Around the Corner

Ratio digital 2D : 4D, sex hormones and behavior

Turn your right or left hand - the left is often clearer if you're right-handed - palm-up. Look carefully at the size of your index finger (2D) and ring finger (4D). If you're a man, there's a good chance that your ring finger is longer than your index finger. And vice versa if you're a woman. If this isn't conclusive, compare the results with your family and friends, and you'll gradually notice average differences depending on whether they're male or female. In the scientific literature, we speak of the 2D:4D ratio, i.e. the length of the index finger divided by the length of the ring finger. This ratio is a feature showing clear sexual dimorphism, with lower average values in males than in females (less than 1 in the former, equal to or greater than 1 in the latter).

The subject may seem trivial, but it has given rise to hundreds of works and even a book by John T. Manning, the world's leading expert on the subject. Manning is the world's leading expert on the subject. For this digital ratio is positively or negatively correlated with a large number of traits, beyond the mere chance of statistical associations. These include: visuospatial abilities, verbal skills, emotionality, aggressiveness, athletic ability in women, homosexuality in Caucasians, birth weight, sperm count per ejaculate, depression, autism and Asperger's syndrome, congenital hyperplasia, obesity, heart disease...

But where do these diverse associations come from? The prevailing hypothesis is that the 2D:4D ratio is largely determined during pregnancy, by the influence of sex hormones on developmental genes. The more the fetus is bathed in testosterone, the more likely its ring finger is to be long, and thus correspond to a male digital ratio. The opposite would be true for estradiol, a female hormone. However, the trait has a continuous variation: men can have a female ratio and women a male ratio.

A team led by Svetlana Lutchmaya (University of Cambridge) has recently, and for the first time, attempted to verify this association directly. She analyzed 33 pregnancies (18 boys, 15 girls) in detail, with precise assessments of testosterone and estradiol levels during routine amniocentesis and no less precise measurement of the digital ratio at two years of age. Result: whatever the sex of the children, there was a significant correlation between the testosterone/estradiol ratio and the 2D:4D ratio. This study therefore supports the hormonal hypothesis on the configuration of the digital ratio. But also, by extension, the other correlations found by the researchers: our index and ring fingers could be serious clues to the way our brains have been "masculinized" or "feminized" during our uterine development.

Fortune-tellers claim to read our destiny in the lines of our hands. Perhaps they should add the length of our fingers to their predictive panoply.

References

S. Lutchmaya *et al* (2004), "2nd to 4th digit ratios, fetal testosterone and estradiol", *Early Human Development*, 77, 23-28.

J. T. Manning (2002), *Digit Ratio. A pointer to Fertility, Behavior and Health*, New Jersey, Rutgers University Press.

PART FIVE

Menstrual Cycle, Sexual Cycle

The Cuckold's Tactic

Ovulatory period and sexual capture strategy

The writer Paul Léautaud, a great optimist before the eternal, used to say that betrayal is second nature to women. According to the very broad statistics of paternity tests, between 1% and 30% of children are not the sons or daughters of their supposed fathers. Rates vary enormously from country to country and from method to method. Above all, they are difficult to control, as no large population has ever been fully analyzed, for ethical reasons. By definition, paternity tests are often carried out when there are serious doubts. The credible values most often put forward are at the very bottom of the range, between 1 and 5%. This still means that one child in 100 to one child in 20 was conceived with a lover.

As ever, Darwinian evolutionary theory is not short of hypotheses on the phenomenon of infidelity. In particular, it predicts that women will tend to be more fickle during the fertile phase of their sexual cycle. And that men, for their part, will tend to be more considerate, even more pressing, during this same phase.

Steven Gangestad's team (University of New Mexico) has tested this hypothesis. Their study involved 51 female students with an average age of 19.6, most of whom were heterosexual (48) or self-declared bisexual (3), but had only had male partners in the past year. Of these students, 31 said they had an official partner, 24 of them exclusive (the others gave no particular details of their degree of monogamy). Of the remaining 20 young women, 14 were virgins, but six had official boyfriends. The remaining six had occasional, non-exclusive partners. At the start of the study, all had not taken any contraception for at least a month. On average, they had had 3.3 partners since the start of their sexual lives. In short, they were perfectly normal girls.

The study consisted of two questionnaires to be completed during the fertile (five days around ovulation) and infertile periods. The first concerned their sexual practices, fantasies and moods. The second looked at their boyfriends' behavior: thoughtfulness, ability to get upset if they saw them walking with another boy, self-congratulation in front of witnesses... In short, once again, the classic behavior of the young male.

The results of the first questionnaire showed that girls are more likely to fantasize about other boys, or even "cheat" on their boyfriends, during the ovulation period, but feel no particular change in desire for their official mates. At the same time, boys' attention to their partners rises by 30% during this fertile phase. They tend to be jealous, possessive or boastful in front of their mates during this same period. From an evolutionary point of view, this means that men develop a capture-retention strategy to dissuade their partners from going elsewhere, at a time when the latter are more likely to compromise the transmission of their genetic heritage. On the other hand, women also tend to consider infidelity during ovulation. Studies on larger samples would of course be welcome.

Tentative conclusion, ladies: if he calls ten times during the day, asks you what you're doing and who you're seeing, cooks you a romantic dinner when you get home, you may well be in the ovulatory phase.

Reference

S. W. Gangestad *et al* (2002), "Changes in women's sexual interests and their partners' mate-retention tactics across the menstrual cycle: evidence for shifting conflicts of interest", *Proceedings of the Royal Society of London, Biological Sciences*, 269, 1494, 975-982.

Michael Jackson or Barry White?

Menstrual cycle and male vocal attractiveness

Male humanity can be classified in many ways. For example, according to the level of testosterone, one of the main male sex hormones. We can also classify behaviors according to this hormone level: men with high testosterone levels are more likely to have a developed sex life, with more than the average number of one-night stands. Conversely, a low testosterone level can induce a tendency towards quiet, hen-dad-like behavior. Women, on the other hand, would have a great advantage if they could identify each type and choose the one that suits them best.

According to David Feinberg of the University of Saint Andrews (Scotland), a researcher specializing in outward signs of masculinity, there is no shortage of predictive hypotheses surrounding these hormonal issues. Such is the case with a deep voice, a known indicator of high testosterone levels. Women may tend to prefer this vocal register when they are in their fertile years. The scientist asked 26 volunteers, aged 18 to 23, heterosexual, without any hormonal contraception for at least three months, with regular cycles and perfect hearing, to listen to vocal samples. These samples came from 4 women and 4 men, then digitally modified and pronounced the phonemes "o", "a", "i", "o" and "é" at 500 ms intervals. The digital modifications concerned pitch and frequency, ranging from 65 to 300 Hz for the male voices, and from 100 to 600 Hz for the female voices. In order to feminize the voices, the scientists increased this frequency by 20 Hz and conversely lowered it by the same frequency to create the male voices. The amplitude of each sample was normalized to 87 dB.

The sound samples were evaluated once a week for 4 to 6 weeks. Each time they completed the questionnaire, participants were asked to provide a urine sample to measure their hormone levels and thus their fertility levels. Information on the menstrual cycle, including the date of menstruation and the length of the cycle, was also collected via a self-administered questionnaire. Sexual orientation was also specified on a scale of 1 to 7 (1 completely homosexual, 7 completely heterosexual).

The volunteers in this experiment had to decide on the quality of the voices and rate them on a double scale of 1 to 7; the first for attractiveness (1 for extremely unattractive and 7 for extremely attractive) and the second for degree of dominance (1 for not very dominant, 7 for very dominant). Female and male voices were scored separately, at random. In the end, 11 women completed the questionnaire once during their fertile period, 12 twice and 2 three times. Two women rated the voices twice during their non-fertile phase, 10 three times and 13 four times.

Result: every time the volunteers gave the highest scores in both attractiveness and dominance, they were in the ovulatory period, and the chosen voices, both male and female, had seen their original frequency lowered (deeper), the correlation being clearer for the male voices.

Will Barry White always be more attractive than Michael Jackson? Not so sure: "The menstrual cycle doesn't influence every woman in the same way," explains Feinberg. While we can legitimately assume that male men will be chosen for one-night stands, our research shows that the most desirable and feminine women can capture these men, and enroll them in long-term relationships. Similarly, while a man with a high-pitched voice isn't doomed to be single, there will always be a risk that his wife will cheat on him with a man with a deeper voice." Nothing is ever simple when it comes to Darwinian sex. One thing's for sure: if you've got a falsetto voice, a beautiful wife and friends with tenor voices, take a few precautions.

Reference

D. R. Feinberg *et al* (2005), "Menstrual cycle, trait estrogen level, and masculinity preferences in the human voice", *Hormones and Behavior*, 49, 215-222.

I can Smell it's You

Male recognition of female fertility

If a woman's ovulation can't be detected visually, can it be olfactory? Research has already shown that human beings are able to rely on certain olfactory cues to recognize their peers, and even to evaluate potential sexual partners. The menstrual cycle is a prime example of this unconscious ability to detect fertile women.

A recent study by Devendra Singh and Matthew Bronstad attempted to test this hypothesis. It involved 17 women of Caucasian origin, with an average age of 22.4, who had to wear a T-shirt for three consecutive nights, at two points in their cycle: the fertile (follicular) phase and the non-fertile (luteal) phase. These women had not been taking hormonal contraception for at least six months and agreed to follow a strict diet in order to produce a neutral odor. They also had to wash only with fragrance-free products, have no sexual relations, sleep strictly alone (no men or animals) during the test, and not even use household products. On a logbook, the volunteers recorded the dates of their periods to determine the fertile phases of their cycle. The T-shirt was enclosed in a standardized plastic bag for the three days it was worn. Once collected, the body-odor-impregnated clothing was frozen.

These T-shirts were then collected in 21 pairs and randomly presented to 52 men of Caucasian origin, with an average age of 23.3. None of the volunteers knew the women who had worn the T-shirts. Participants were asked to rate from 1 to 10 the "pleasant" and "sexy" nature of the T-shirts' scent, as well as its intensity. The protocol was simple: the T-shirts were placed in plastic bags inside standardized boxes, the participants opened the plastic bag without touching the fabric, smelled and then closed it again. The non-fertile phase T-shirts were marked "L" and the fertile phase "F", but none of the participants knew the meaning of these letters.

Result: of the 21 pairs, 17 T-shirts achieved very high scores, and all belonged to women in their fertile phase. The results remained the same after a seven-day transit of the T-shirts in the freezer. For Devendra Singh, the experiment demonstrates that body odor has been selected as a strong signal to indicate female readiness. Even if, in our cultures, these olfactory cues from our distant animal past are now surpassed by make-up, perfume, clothing style or behavior.

Reference

D. Singh and P. M. Bronstad (2001), "Female body odour is a potential cue to ovulation", *Proceedings of the Royal Society of London*, Biological Sciences, 268, 797-801.

THE BEAUTY OF EGGS

Ovulation, body odor and facial beauty

Unlike their primate counterparts, most of whom display turgid vulvas during the fertile period, human females conceal their ovulation. From the outside, the follicular (peri-ovulatory) phase is indistinguishable from the luteal (non-ovulatory) phase of the menstrual cycle. Except perhaps for the moodiness associated with imminent menstruation. The human male therefore seems to have no bearings when it comes to hunting down a fertile female. In fact, a series of recent studies show that this is not entirely true. Subtle cues lead men to prefer women in their fertile phase.

S. Craig Roberts (University of Newcastle) and his team recruited 48 volunteers (23 British, 25 Czech) aged between 19 and 33, with regular 28-day cycles and not taking the pill. These women were photographed twice, once in their follicular phase, once in their luteal phase. In both cases, they adopted the same neutral expression. The photos were taken in a studio, under artificial lighting of identical intensity and orientation. The photographs of these 48 women were placed opposite each other, and the researchers then asked 261 volunteers to judge which face was the most attractive. These volunteers (130 men and 131 women, aged between 19 and 44 for the men and between 18 and 33 for the women) could take as long as they wished to make their judgment, and click on the preferred portrait. The test was carried out twice: first the whole face, then just the face (ears and hair masked).

A random distribution would have given 50-50 for the follicular and luteal phases. But this is not the case. On average, portraits of women in the fertile phase are preferred to portraits of women in the sterile phase. Thus, 53% of men and 58% of women express a preference for the faces of fertile women. The difference is not huge, of course, but it is statistically significant. The researchers have not yet identified the traits involved in this preference. They suspect that sex hormones vary lip size and color, skin tone and pupil dilation. It's worth noting that women's judgment is more pronounced in favor of their fertile counterparts than that of men. This may mean that women are simply more attentive to certain details of their bodies. Or that competition between women for access to sexual partners throughout evolution has sharpened their recognition of potential competitors.

Facial beauty isn't the only external cue that changes with the rhythm of the menstrual cycle: the same goes for body odour (see *above*, "It smells like you"). It is by no means certain that the sensitivity to female ovulation of people living in the most frustrated conditions is better than that of modernized societies (less bodily hygiene, no cosmetics). Anthropologist Frank W. Marlowe, for example, investigated the Hadza (African hunter-gatherers living in Tanzania), to find out whether they make the link between sex and reproduction on the one hand, and whether they know when a woman is most fertile on the other. The first point is proven, but not the second: the Hadza believe that a woman is most fertile just after her period, as was the case in the West before the 19th century.

References

F. W. Marlowe (2004), "Is human ovulation concealed? Evidence from conception beliefs in a hunter-gatherer society", *Archives of Sexual Behavior*, 33, 427-432.

S. C. Roberts *et al.* (2004), "Female facial attractiveness increases during the fertile phase of the menstrual cycle", *Proceedings of the Royal Society of London, Biological Sciences*, 271, S270-S272.

D. Singh and P. M. Bronstad (2001), "Female body odour is a potential cue to ovulation", *Proceedings of the Royal Society of London, Biological Sciences*, 268, 797-801.

Macho Awakening in the Fertile Phase

Male competition and female fertility

As we noted earlier, women are slightly more likely to cheat on their husbands during the ovulation phase. But are they condemned to cuckoldry, or can they sense this infidelity? According to a study by Rob Burriss and Anthony Little, males have an instinctive defense against their competitors.

First, 11 men, with an average age of 26.18, were chosen to judge the dominance of 66 male photos on a scale of 1 to 7. Dominance is broadly and pragmatically defined here as "being able to get what you want". The photos were then ranked in descending order of dominance scores. Using computer morphing, the researchers created 22 composite photos: the first based on the three faces deemed most dominant, the last on the least dominant trio, with the others ranging to varying degrees between the extremes. These 22 photos were then presented to 64 heterosexual men, of Caucasian origin, living in couples and with an average age of 28.58. The volunteers were not informed of the purpose of the study and were volunteers. Their current sexual partners were classified into two groups, according to their menstrual cycle phase at the time of the study: 33 at high risk of fertilization and 31 at low risk. In each group, 16 women were taking hormonal contraception. Questionnaires focused on the degree of photo dominance, defined in the same way as for the first group used to develop the composites.

The results showed that men whose partners were in the first high-risk group judged the faces in the composite photos to be more dominant on average. Men whose partners were on the pill and/or in the low-ovulatory-risk group, on the other hand, saw the composites as expressing less dominance. This judgement was valid irrespective of the actual dominance (strong or weak) of the composite portraits.

For Rob Burriss, these results come as no surprise: "Like chimpanzees, we're social animals and relatively peaceful most of the time, but when a female becomes fertile, two dominant males may come to fight for her attention and thus spread their genes. Similarly, the judgment of dominance increases when the female is the most fertile. What's interesting is to see how men's behavior is influenced by women's physiological data: men become more wary of other men at the same time as evaluation of virile-typed faces changes in pre-ovulatory women." According to the scientist, dads have everything to fear from cads: "Men with big eyes, round cheeks or full lips - in short, those who are judged to be more feminine - are more often chosen to be long-term partners. And they're not considered dominant." So it's these men who have the most to worry about when their partners ovulate. The latter may well take advantage of their good parental investment while choosing to reproduce the genes of another, more dominant male. The warning signal for this risk seems to exist. Whether it's always enough remains to be seen. Household peace is not for tomorrow.

Reference

R. P. Burriss and A. C. Little (2006), "Effects of partner conception risk phase on male perception of dominance in faces", *Evolution and Human Behavior*, 27, 297-305.

The Pill against Darwin?

Hormonal contraception and changes in partner choice

If women's sexual choices vary according to their hormonal state, we can predict that they will be altered by oral contraception or pregnancy. According to a study led by psychologist Anthony C. Little, the contraceptive pill does influence partner selection. To arrive at this conclusion, the research team brought together five different analyses, on population samples of appreciable size.

The first study involved 639 British women, aged between 20 and 25, who reported having regular cycles. The questionnaire asked them to rate 4 pairs of photos of male faces, each pair comprising two versions of a "basic face" digitally modified to correspond to either high or low testosterone levels. Faces with the masculine markers of high testosterone levels are assumed to be "healthier" than others, as testosterone is known to have a significant immunosuppressive effect in males, both human and other species. Enduring high levels of the male hormone would therefore be indicative of a "strong" immune system.

The color images were composed from the photographs of 80 Caucasian men aged 18 to 30. Participants were then asked to rate their liking using a 4-item MCQ: indifferent, weak preference, neutral, strong. They were also asked to state their sexual orientation, the date of their last menstrual period, their contraceptive method, their marital status and whether they were pregnant. In all cases, the faces modified to appear most testosterone-revealing were the most selected, but this selection was even more pronounced during the fertile phase.

The second series involved the assessment of male and female faces. The 30 new participants, heterosexual female students aged 18 to 23, who had not been on contraception for at least three months and were not pregnant, were confronted with 12 new pairs of faces (6 female and 6 male), composed to correspond to different degrees of apparent health. The questionnaires lasted six weeks, and each time the volunteers were asked to provide a urine sample to determine the follicular phase they were in. The result: a greater attraction to faces with a high (healthy) testosterone index, regardless of gender, during the participants' fertile period.

The third study, involving 31 volunteers similar to the previous study, involved 6 new pairs of faces, composed in the same way as in the first research. The questionnaires were to be completed over a four-week period, and focused on the choice of a short- or long-term relationship. The faces were presented randomly, interspersed with control images. In this case, women in a fertile phase were more likely to choose masculinized faces for short-term, but not long-term, relationships.

In the fourth study, 115 pregnant women were shown the photos from the first study and asked to evaluate them in the same way. Opposite them, 857 non-pregnant women without oral contraception acted as a test group. As in studies 1 and 3, the maximum number of responses went to the most clearly masculine faces.

Finally, in the last study, 1,570 heterosexual women on the pill and 1,325 off the pill were presented with the faces from studies 1 and 4, again using the same evaluation methods. On average, all these women expressed a stronger attraction to testosterone-marked faces, but this preference was stronger in the women on the pill.

So, if sexual choice varies according to the ovarian cycle, it also varies according to the nature of the desired relationship, whether short-term (more common in women using contraception and not wishing to start a family) or long-term (in which case less virile features would be a guarantee of lasting parental investment). Beware, however, of what happens next, warns Little: "A woman who chose her man while under the influence of the pill may find she got the wrong husband once she wants children and he raises them." In other words, modern contraception could well upset the rules of sexual selection, making people prefer "good fertilizers" when they are not fertile, and regret "good investors" when they have reproduced. Could the pill be a little-known factor behind the dizzying rise in divorce rates?

Reference

B. C. Jones *et al.* (2005), "Menstrual cycle, pregnancy and oral contraceptive use alter attraction to apparent health in faces", *Proceedings of the Royal Society of London*, Biological Sciences, 272, 347-354.

You're Uglier when I Ovulate

Sexual competition in fertile women

Did Darwinism convey certain cultural or sexual prejudices? Possibly, since its founder lived in the prudish Victorian era. A good example concerns theories of sexual selection: for a long time, they focused on men's competition for women, as if it were self-evident that women were passive objects of sexuality. Over the last thirty years or so, this prejudice has been shattered, and we now know that competition between females also plays an important role in the history of living organisms. Moreover, as Leigh Van Valen has shown, sexual selection obeys the principle of the Red Queen, the character in *The Other Side of the Looking Glass* (sequel to *Alice in Wonderland*) who runs faster and faster to stay in the same place. When a trait begins to be selected, the phenomenon self-amplifies: generation after generation, predators run faster, and so do their prey. Until an equilibrium is reached. The same thing happens in the sexual domain: if men prefer certain beauty traits, women will tend to accentuate them. And to depreciate their competitors in this respect.

University of Toronto psychologist Maryanne Fisher asked 57 heterosexual female students, average age 19, to give their opinions on 30 photos of men and 35 photos of women. The participants, who had not been taking any hormonal contraceptives for at least three months and claimed to have regular cycles, were then divided into two groups according to the time of their ovulatory cycle. The models for these photos were students from previous years whom the participants were not supposed to know, so as not to be influenced in their judgement. The pictures were in color, all made on the same model: black clothes, no distinguishing marks (glasses, jewelry) and neutral facial expression. Participants were asked to view the photos, projected randomly on a computer screen, and judge them on a scale of 1 to 7 (1 for extremely unattractive, 7 for extremely attractive). Speed of response was also measured. A test group of 47 men, average age 21, followed the same procedure and formed the study's test sample.

Overall, women found photos of women more attractive (3.43) than photos of men (2.41). However, students between the 12th and 21st day of their menstrual cycle, with higher estrogen levels, rated female photos as uglier than others. During the same period, appreciation of male figures did not change significantly. Although the female photos were looked at slightly longer than the male ones, the researcher noted no significant difference in response time according to ovulatory phase.

During the fertile period, potential competitors thus sharpen their contempt and belittling judgment. Estrogen may also have an influence on mood and positive self-perception - it's also known that these hormones have a real influence on the freshness of complexion, lip color and shine of hair. The preconceived notion that women are attentive to others or reluctant to compete may well cease to be valid when it comes to matters of the heart and the bedroom. Here again, we're extending the realm of the struggle.

Reference

M. L. Fisher (2004), "Female intrasexual competition decreases female facial attractiveness", *Proceedings of the Royal Society of London*, series B, supplement, Biology Letters, 283-285. DOI 10.1098/rsbl.2004.0160.

PART SIX

THE ORIGINS OF THE GAY GENUS

IN SEARCH OF GAY GENES

Genetic basis of homosexuality

In 1993, the news made headlines around the world: the gene for homosexuality had been discovered. As usual, shortcuts were the order of the day. Dean Hamer, then a researcher at the US National Institutes of Health (NIH), and his team had identified a genetic marker on the X chromosome (locus Xq28), found slightly more frequently in male homosexuals than in the rest of the population. A marker is not, strictly speaking, a gene, but rather a small writing variation within a gene. In any case, the affair caused quite a stir, and the hunt for homosexual genes was on.

Dean Hamer's team's initial discovery of the Xq28 marker led to several replication attempts. The same laboratory succeeded in 1995 (Hu *et al.*), but this was not the case a few years later for two other independent teams (Rice *et al.* in 1999, Sanders and Dawood in 2003). Comparing these four studies, we used a common statistical method in genomics (Multiple Scan Probability) to assess the relevance of the association: the result was 0.0003, i.e. not very conclusive. Further work on candidate genes on the X chromosome (AR) or chromosome 15 (CYP19A1) also failed to produce results.

Is the gay gene a myth and is homosexuality only acquired during our development? This is doubtful. To find out whether a trait or behavior has a genetic basis, researchers carry out heritability studies. They compare identical twins (sharing 100% of their nuclear genes) with fraternal twins (sharing only 50%) and look at the results. Since monozygotic and dizygotic twins developed together in the womb and were subsequently raised together, they are very similar in terms of environment. If there is a marked difference on a given trait - for example, if identical twins are on average more often both homosexual than are fraternal twins - there is good reason to suspect that genes partly influence the behavior studied. And they do. The two most important analyses of this question were carried out on the Australian twin registry, with 1,538 and 1,405 pairs of twins respectively. Both found similar, fairly high heritabilities (0.51 and 0.58 for male homosexuality, 0.23 and 0.21 for female homosexuality). And these results replicate those already found on slightly smaller cohorts (Bailey, 2000; Kirk, 2000).

If there's heritability, it's because there are genes. But we still have to find them. Since the 1990s and the start of molecular analyses of homosexuality, we know that genomics has made immense progress. The human genome and those of many other species have been sequenced. Advances in bioinformatics, sequencers and DNA chips have made it possible to work ever more rapidly on large numbers of genes and individuals. Brian Mustanki's team (University of Illinois, Chicago) took advantage of these advances to analyze the entire genome, rather than just the X chromosome or regions of susceptibility. The researchers gathered a sample of 456 individuals from 146 different families. Of these families, 137 had two homosexual brothers, and 9 had three brothers of the same orientation. The researchers then refined this sample by distinguishing between families with heterosexual siblings and those where X chromosome transmission was known (the Y chromosome is always transmitted by the father, but the X chromosome is paternal or maternal).

The result of this new work: three specific regions have been identified in homosexual subjects on chromosomes 7 (7q36), 8 (8p12) and 10 (10q26). The genes concerned could be the vasoactive peptide type 2 receptor (which influences brain construction) and the gonagotropin 1 control hormone (which influences the expression of sex hormones), as well as an active zone on chromosome 10 comprising several genes known to be sensitive to maternal imprinting (i.e. transmission does not follow classical Mendelian laws, with gene expression being favored according to the transmitting parent). The Xq28 marker was not found in this new study.

"Our research helps establish that genes play an important role in determining whether a man is gay or heterosexual," says B. S. Mustanski. "We still need to confirm this work and identify the specific genes linked to sexual orientation within these chromosomal sequences." It's certainly a long-term project. In recent years, for example, over a hundred genes linked to the production of the nervous system have been identified, whose expression varies during embryonic development in men and women. This shows that the "sexualization" of the brain and behavior is not simply a retroactive effect of hormones, but concerns the genome itself.

The quest for gay genes therefore has a bright future ahead of it. Of course, it will only explain half the story, since sexual orientation depends just as much on the life choices made by individuals over the course of their lives.

References

J. M. Bailey *et al* (2000), "Genetic and environmental influences on sexual orientation and its correlates in an Australian twin sample", *Journal of Personality and Social Psychology*, 78, 524-536.

D. H. Hamer *et al* (1993), "A linkage between DNA markers on the X chromosome and male sexual orientation", *Science*, 261, 320-326.

K. M. Kirk *et al* (2000), "Measurement models for sexual orientation in a community twin sample", *Behavior Genetics*, 30, 345-356.

B. S. Mustanski *et al* (2005), "A genomewide scan of male sexual orientation", *Human Genetics*, 116, 272-278.

ARE HOMOSEXUALS LEFT-WING?

Manual laterality and sexual orientation

In every human population, there are right-handers and left-handers. The former represent the vast majority (83-90%), the latter a small minority (8-15%). To these must be added those with varying degrees of ambidexterity or ill-defined dominance (2%), although true ambidexterity - the ability to do everything in the same way with the right and left hand - is extremely rare. On average, men are slightly more left-handed than women.

As their name implies, left-handed people have been frowned upon in many societies: they are "left-handed" (unskillful), if not "sinister" (a depreciative evolution of the Latin word *sinister*, "left-handed"). Straight", conversely, is valued. Until recently, some families preferred to upset people who were left-handed from birth. If our ancestors had read our epidemiological statistics, they might have been confirmed in their prejudices: being left-handed isn't very good for your health, and has been associated (statistically) with a higher probability of developing mental and immune disorders, miscarriages, serious accidents, low birth weights and, to put it bluntly, a shorter life expectancy. However, left-handed people can rest assured that the additional risk is real, but statistically very small. And correlations are not causalities.

Like left-handed people, homosexuals were frowned upon in some societies. But this analogy is obviously not the origin of the scientific questioning on this subject. In the early 1980s, neuropsychologist J. Lindsay suggested that homosexuals were more left-handed than the general population. Subsequently, this observation has been the subject of a large number of studies, with samples and methodologies of widely varying quality. To find out for sure, Martin L. Lalumière and his colleagues at the University of Toronto carried out a meta-analysis, i.e. a qualitative and quantitative comparison of all previous work on the subject. Their work brought together twenty studies comparing 6,987 homosexuals (6,182 men, 805 women) and 16,423 heterosexuals (14,808 men, 1,615 women).

Result: the imbalance of manual laterality in relation to sexual orientation is a reality. Homosexual men are 39% more likely than heterosexuals to be non-right-handed (i.e. left-handed, ambidextrous or with undefined dominance). Among homosexual women, the verdict is clear: 91% more likely. This imbalance is difficult to explain by environmental factors: upbringing or culture may influence homosexuality or laterality, but hardly the link between the two. What's more, ultrasound scans show that manual laterality is already determined in the womb, with the thumb sucked by the fetus in 95% of cases being that of its future dominant hand.

At least three hypotheses have been put forward to explain the link between laterality and homosexuality. The first is hormonal: sex hormones are known to influence the lateralization of the brain, prior to that of the hands. But this doesn't exactly fit with the results: gays are supposed to be underexposed to testosterone in the womb, lesbians overexposed. In this case, gays would be more right-handed (a more feminine trait). On the other hand, the hormonal hypothesis works well with lesbians, since being left-handed is a slightly more masculine trait. Another possibility is the immune response. It is suspected that sexual orientation is influenced by the mother's immune response to her fetus, in particular to antigens linked to the Y chromosome (for male embryos). If genes involved in laterality are also subject to the effect of maternal antibodies, we can explain the imbalance in males, but not in females this time. Third and most general hypothesis: developmental instability. Left-handedness, as we have seen, is associated with slight physiological imbalances in the general plane of body symmetry, perhaps due to an early expression of certain developmental genes, resulting in more frequent illnesses and accidents. The imbalance in sexual preferences (relative to the species average) would be just one expression of this initial instability.

There's no shortage of speculation, but none of it is currently conclusive. Finally, a word of encouragement for homosexual and heterosexual left-handers alike, perhaps worried by these cold descriptions of their supposed imbalances: studies have also shown that left-handers possess some advantages over the rest of the population in face-to-face combat, in many sports (from baseball to tennis), in certain creative fields, and even in average income levels, when compared with right-handers in equivalent studies.

Reference

M. L. Lalumière *et al* (2000), "Sexual orientation and handedness in men and women. A meta-analysis", *Psychological Bulletin*, 126, 575-592.

Mothers and Aunts

Adaptive benefits of homosexuality

Bonobos kissing, manatees rubbing, beetles mounting, koalas, foxes, elephants, ducks in full romp... the spectacle of love is everywhere in nature. Except that these tender scenes involve individuals of the same sex. They were reported (and illustrated) by Bruce Bagemihl, zoologist and champion of the gay cause, author of a best-selling book on homosexuality in the animal world (Bagemihl, 1999). Homosexual scenes range from touching to fellatio and from cunnilingus to penetration. "Animal homosexuality is by no means a new discovery of modern science", explains the author: it has been known since Antiquity. In the meantime, Christianity had, of course, cast a discreet and theological veil over these "unnatural" relationships... which turned out to be quite natural!

Bagemihl's book has been challenged on certain details by specialists, not least because of its overly broad definition of homosexuality - mere genital stimulation from time to time does not mean a lasting, exclusive relationship with a partner of the same sex. But the fact remains, and it's even more indisputable in the human species: not all individuals are naturally "programmed" to find happiness in love with a partner of the opposite sex.

Homosexuality poses an interesting problem for evolutionary theory. By definition, only an individual's advantageous traits are passed on to the next generation (if they have a genetic basis). Homosexuality cannot be advantageous from this point of view, since it does not lead to reproduction. So, if homosexuality has a genetic basis, it should have died out long ago in the face of competition from heterosexual genes, which are by nature more prolific. However, this is not the case, and all the evidence points to the existence of genes associated with sexual orientation (see "In search of gay genes" above).

How can this paradox be resolved? Several avenues have been proposed. Edward Wilson, the father of sociobiology, suggested that homosexuals might be more altruistic towards their heterosexual relatives: failing to pass on their own genes directly, they would indirectly help to do so by increasing the chances of survival of their relatives (who, by definition, partly possess the genes concerned). But subsequent studies have not shown that homosexuals are on average more prone to familial altruism than others.

Another possibility is pleiotropy. Behind this barbaric name lies a fairly simple definition: the same gene can have several effects, and positive effects can counterbalance negative ones. A classic example: the same gene that causes sickle-cell anemia (a hemoglobin disease) provides a certain degree of protection against malaria, depending on whether it is homozygous (a single copy, beneficial effect) or heterozygous (two copies, deleterious effect). This gene therefore persists in populations where malaria is rife, since it has an advantage when a single copy comes from one of its parents. Mutatis mutandis, the same could be said of the many genes involved in sexual orientation.

On paper, this is an interesting hypothesis. But what happens in reality? The first empirical proof of this phenomenon was recently provided by an Italian team led by Andrea Camperio-Ciani (University of Padua).

The researchers asked 98 homosexual males and 100 heterosexual males to fill in a fairly detailed questionnaire about their family: brothers and sisters, cousins, uncles and aunts, grandparents. In all, they obtained information on over 4,600 people from the subjects' maternal and paternal lines. The result: maternal lineages are more fertile in homosexuals than in heterosexuals, a difference not found in paternal lineages. For example: mothers of homosexuals have an average of 2.69 children versus 2.32; maternal aunts 1.98 versus 1.51; maternal grandmothers 3.55 versus 3.39. This systematic advantage is not reflected in the paternal equivalents, which are randomly distributed.

The researchers' conclusion: certain genes that predispose to homosexuality in men, and that are passed down through maternal lines only, confer greater fertility on women. The genes in question are probably on the X chromosome. And this adaptive advantage would explain 14% of the variance in the probability of being gay or straight. If replicated on larger samples, this study will be the first demonstration of the important pleiotropic effect of sexual orientation genes in human evolution. It would also explain why the homosexual minority

has never disappeared from our societies, even when perse-
cuted or condemned by the majority.

References

B. Bagemihl (1999), Biological Exuberance. Animal Homosexuality and Natural Diversity, New York, St. Martin's Press.

A. Camperio-Ciani *et al* (2004), "Evidence for maternally inherited factors favouring male homosexuality and promoting female fecundity", *Proceedings of the Royal Society of London, Biological Sciences*, 271, 2217-2221.

THE BAND OF BROTHERS

Homosexuality and sibling birth order

Sigmund Freud hypothesized that family relationships had an early influence on the development of sexuality. The founder of psychoanalysis was interested in the symbolic relationships between children and their parents. If he had wanted to understand homosexuality, which he analyzed rather negatively as a halt in sexual development, Freud should have been more interested in brothers and sisters. A vast body of research indicates that birth order has a significant influence on sexual orientation.

Canadian psychologist Ray Blanchard (Department of Psychiatry, University of Toronto) has been studying this question for some twenty years, along with his colleague Anthony F. Bogaert of Brock University. In 2001, Blanchard published a synthesis of work on the relationship between male homosexuality and birth order. He reviewed 14 studies on the subject, carried out in the 1990s alone, comparing the family structures of several thousand subjects declared to be homosexual or heterosexual. The verdict is clear: in all the studies, the presence of older brothers significantly increased the probability of homosexuality for the younger sibling, a phenomenon not found with older sisters. For each older brother, this probability increases by 33%. The figure may seem huge, but it really isn't, as Ray Blanchard reminds journalists who suggest that some homophobic mothers might choose to have abortions after having two or three sons: if the probability of being homosexual in a population is 2% (0.020), an increase of 33% only ever raises it to 0.027, and you need more than five older brothers to approach 0.1 (one chance in ten).

Nevertheless, sibling birth rank is the most important relative predisposing factor to homosexuality identified to date. Above 2.5 brothers (a statistical value, of course, as half-brothers are rare in life), it would explain more than half of all declared homosexualities. The first reflex, in the Freudian manner, is obviously to think that older brothers influence their younger siblings during childhood: a child raised in a male environment would be more likely to be homosexual. But this is not the case. In a recent study, Anthony F. Bogaert compared 944 homosexuals and heterosexuals with either biological or non-biological older brothers (adopted or from the father's first marriage): the sibling birth order only had an effect in the first case. It is indeed when the mother has borne male children that the probability increases with each new birth. If environment has an influence, it's the uterine environment, not the family environment.

How can this disturbing discovery be explained? The strongest hypothesis to date concerns the mother's immune response. A quick reminder: when a foetus develops in the mother's womb, it represents a partial foreign body, particularly as it contains half of the father's genes. This is why there are so many natural miscarriages in the early stages. As a rule, however, the mother's immune system eventually tolerates the presence of the fetus, and rejection during advanced pregnancy is fortunately rare (pre-eclampsia). Nevertheless, immune cells develop antibodies against fetal elements crossing the placental barrier into the mother's bloodstream. This is logically the case for proteins derived from the male child's Y chromosome, since the mother lacks this Y chromosome. In a subsequent pregnancy, these antibodies, still present in the mother's immune system, more readily recognize a new male foetus as an "intruder" in the home. The response becomes stronger each time. And the influence more noticeable. In particular, it concerns the minor histocompatibility complex (H-Y antigens) expressed by men. And, more generally, the processes of intra-uterine development of the nervous system linked to sex chromosomes.

If this hypothesis is correct, as suggested by a number of rodent experiments and clues such as the lower birth weight of male cadets, then the sexual orientation of the brain would be shaped by the mother at the very origins of existence. Freud was wrong in his interpretation, but perhaps not wrong in his intuitions: the relationship with the mother is a key element in understanding human sexuality.

References

R. Blanchard (2001), "Fraternal birth order and the maternal immune hypothesis of male homosexuality", *Hormones and Behavior*, 40, 2, 105-114.

A. F. Bogaert (2004), "The prevalence of male homosexuality. The effect of fraternal birth order and variations in family size", *Journal of Theoretical Biology*, 230, 33-37.

A. F. Bogaert (2006), "Biological versus nonbiological older brothers and men's sexual orientation", *Proceedings of the National Academy of Sciences (PNAS)*, 103, 28, 10771-10774.

A Tough Nut

Brain differences and sexual orientation

Simon LeVay now lives in West Hollywood, California, in active retirement, writing popular scientific articles and books. His 1993 essay, *The Sexual Brain*, is one of the most influential of that famous "brain decade" (1990-2000) which changed the way researchers and the general public alike think about the black box under our skulls.

LeVay is also one of the pioneers of the neurobiological study of homosexuality. In an often-quoted article from 1991, he was the first to hypothesize neuroanatomical differences between the brains of homosexuals and heterosexuals. Given the influence of genes, hormones and life experiences on the configuration of our neurons, the perspective seems fairly coherent. Nevertheless, it caused a minor scandal at the time, with many fearing that we were locking individuals into the immutable constraints of their biological determinations. Since then, people have calmed down, and today, with a few exceptions, we take a more detached view of the vast scientific undertaking to gain an intimate understanding of the human being.

The brain zone of interest highlighted by Simon LeVay in his seminal research has a name that's hard for the layman to remember or even pronounce: the third interstitial nucleus of the anterior hypothalamus. We prefer its English acronym, INAH-3. The hypothalamus is a small region of functional neuronal nuclei buried in the ancient depths of our brain, known as the "limbic system". It plays a fundamental role, since one of its functions is to link the nervous and endocrine systems, neurons and hormones. In other words, the nuclei of the hypothalamus are in constant demand: hunger, thirst, biological rhythms, body temperature and emotions all pass through this pathway. As does sexuality.

The hypothalamus is known to differ between men and women, with the most significant differences being in the pre-optic area. But almost every region of these tiny nuclei is affected, not least by the ebb and flow of our sex hormones. By autopsying brains, Simon LeVay demonstrated that INAH-3 is twice as developed in men as in women, and twice as developed in heterosexual men as in homosexual men. Or, to put it another way, INAH-3 in homosexual males is more similar to that in females than in males. This region is of some importance, since numerous animal studies have shown that it plays a decisive role in sexual arousal.

A subsequent study (Byne, 2001) only partially replicated LeVay's discovery. Using a fairly small number of subjects (14 homosexuals versus 34 heterosexuals), this work confirmed that there is a (non-significant) trend towards a smaller volume of

INAH-3 in gays, but no significant difference in the total number of neurons in the area. Quantity is one thing, but quality? Another recent study, based on a very different methodology, used brain imaging to observe the hypothalamic response to Prozac in homosexuals and heterosexuals. The well-known antidepressant acts on a neurotransmitter, serotonin. Serotonin plays an important role in the hypothalamic circuit and is known to influence sexual behavior. That's why antidepressants often cause breakdowns. The result of this work led by Lean H. Kinnunen: the brains of homosexuals did indeed react less than those of hero-sexuals, indicating that neurochemical circuits don't work quite the same way.

Research into the links between brain anatomy and sexual orientation is still in its infancy, with results sometimes difficult to replicate on small samples. Exploratory techniques are expensive, and homosexuality has fortunately ceased to be a public health problem since it was removed from medical psychiatry in the 1970s. These two factors explain the slow pace of progress. So we'll have to wait a little longer to discover all the secrets of the gay brain.

References

W. Byne *et al* (2001), "The interstitial nuclei of the human anterior hypothalamus: an investigation of variation with sex, sexual orientation, and HIV status", *Hormones and Behavior*, 40, 2, 86-92.

L. H. Kinnunen *et al* (2004), "Differential brain activation in exclusively homosexual and heterosexual men produced by the selective serotonin reuptake inhibitor, fluoxetine", *Brain Research*, 1024, 1-2, 251-254.

S. LeVay (1991), "A difference in hypothalamic structure between heterosexual and homosexual men", *Science*, 253, 1034-1037.

I Don't Feel It

Body odor, pheromones and homosexuality

As we saw in a previous chapter of this book, odors and pheromones still play a role in human heterosexuality. Does this hold true when it comes to the behavior of the Homo genus?

The first study on the subject, led by Charles Wysocki and Yolanda Martins (Monell Center for the Chemical Senses, Philadelphia), involved 82 subjects, male and female, homosexual and heterosexual. They were asked to judge 24 different body odors: T-shirts worn by other subjects, also divided according to gender and orientation. Every possible combination was considered. The result: gays and lesbians showed different preferences from straight volunteers. Those who stood out most clearly were the male homosexuals, both in terms of the odors they preferred and those they emitted. Gays showed a preference for other gays or heterosexual women, but not for straight men, who were the least appreciated. Conversely, the smell of gay men came last on average when judged by others, including straight or lesbian women. As for the smell itself, it was its pleasant or unpleasant character that was the determining criterion, not its intensity. Lesbians, for their part, found a slight preference for feminine smells, but in a statistically less significant way.

In a second study published the same year, a Swedish team led by Ivanka Savic and Hans Berglund (Department of Neuroscience, Stockholm University) developed a more precise protocol. This time, the odors were derived from two molecules considered to be good candidates for human pheromones: two steroids derived from testosterone (AND) and estrogen (EST), found in men's sweat (AND) and women's urine (EST). This time, 36 subjects were involved in the experiment: 12 heterosexual men, 12 heterosexual women and 12 homosexual men. Their brains were examined by positron emission tomography, to see the differences in activated areas and intensity of activation. Common (non-corporeal) odors were also used as a control experiment. Result: gay men reacted in a comparable way to straight women, i.e. the nuclei of their hypothalamus, known to be linked to sexual behavior, were more activated by male (AND) than female (EST) pheromones. Heterosexuals, on the other hand, showed the expected reactions, i.e. a more marked response to the odors of the opposite sex.

In 2006, the same team of Swedish neurobiologists repeated the experiment, but with 12 lesbian volunteers. Again, the results were positive. Homosexual women more often analyzed men's odors via neuronal pathways specific to non-corporeal odors (amygdala and different areas of the cortex), whereas female pheromones more specifically activated hypothalamic nuclei, associated with sexual behavior.

Odors and pheromones are therefore very much dependent on the sexual orientation of both those who emit them and those who perceive them. If you can't smell someone of the same sex as you, it may be a problem of sexual orientation.

References

H. Berglund *et al* (2006), "Brain response to putative pheromones in lesbian women", *Proceedings of the National Academy of Sciences* (*PNAS*), 103, 8269-8274.

Y. Martins *et al.* (2005), "Preference for human body odors is influenced by gender and sexual orientation", *Psychological Science*, 16, 694-701.

I. Savic *et al* (2005), "Brain response to putative pheromones in homosexual men", *Proceedings of the National Academy of Sciences* (*PNAS*), 102, 7356-7361.

Exotic, Erotic

Temperaments, environments and sexual choices

The gene for this has been discovered, the hormone for that has been identified... The press often reports on scientific advances in a rapid, even cursory manner, lacking the space to explain the ins and outs of the advances in question. As a result, the uninformed reader sometimes gets the wrong idea, imagining that this gene or that hormone dictates the behavior of individuals. Things are obviously more complex than this simplified cause-and-effect link. These molecules first produce other molecules. The effect on behavior is indirect. On the question of sexual orientation, as on others, the biological approach is always complementary to a sociocultural approach.

The work of Daryl J. Bem, a social psychologist at Cornell University, is a good illustration of this complementarity. Over the past few years, he has been developing a theory that he calls "Exotic Becomes Erotic" (EBE). What's it all about? Bem's thinking is based on a common-sense observation: finding biological correlates of homosexuality (genes, hormones, neurons, etc.) is one thing, explaining how an individual becomes homosexual quite another. When we ask gays and lesbians about their life trajectory, over two-thirds of them testify that they felt "different" from childhood onwards. Digging deeper, we discover that homosexuals experience "gender non-conformity" in their social, recreational and cultural activities from a very early age. In other words, they don't fit the stereotypes of their sex - the little boy who plays soccer, the little girl who puts make-up on her doll.

This difference, noted in childhood, is not directly sexual: it's more a question of differences in temperament between individuals (which have a biological basis), leading to differences in behavior in relation to others, objects, motivations or actions. How do (exotic) behavioral differences become sexual (erotic)? Studies show that in Western societies, the first memories of sexual attraction to another person date back on average to the age of 10-10.5. These are conscious phenomena (declared memories) and do not prejudge prior, non-conscious processes. But what is it that attracts children? The people most opposed to them, perceived as the most different, i.e. people of the opposite sex. As Daryl Bem reminds us, the popular adage that "opposites attract" doesn't hold true for most of the factors analyzed in couples - on the contrary, on average, people tend to pair up with individuals of the same race, IQ, social level and so on. But there is one area where opposites attract: sex. It's even the basis of heterosexuality, so obvious as to be unthinkable.

Daryl Bem's logic explains how the exotic becomes erotic. The brain would be programmed to recognize from childhood as different, and therefore sexually attractive, people whose behavior is far removed from its own. But if, like some gays and lesbians, we ourselves develop behavior far removed from the norm for our sex, our attraction is reversed. A number of emotional and sexual experiences with same-sex partners can subsequently crystallize boys' or girls' sexual orientation towards exclusive preferences for same-sex partners.

The EBE theory is of course speculative at this stage, and deserves more prediction and quantification than Daryl Bem can offer. But it does have the merit of showing that the opposition between biological determinism (everything is in the genes) and social constructivism (everything is in the environment) is sterile. We always become what we are. But often by circuitous routes.

References

D. J. Bem (1996), "Exotic becomes erotic. A developmental theory of sexual orientation", *Psychological Review*, 103, 320-335.

D. J. Bem (2000), "Exotic becomes erotic. Interpreting the biological correlates of sexual orientation", *Archives of Sexual Behavior*, 29, 6, 531-548.

SEVENTH SKY

ODDS AND ENDS

The Future of Porn Chic

Influence of gender on ad recall

The vogue for "porno chic" has invaded advertising since the early 2000s. The fact that women (and increasingly men too) are more often nude in advertising clips than in real life has not escaped anyone's notice. Porn chic represents a further step in the voyeurism of the spectator-consumer: the exposure of women in suggestive attitudes, associated with erotic practices supposedly deviant or rare compared to the norm, such as sado-masochism, swinging or striptease.

In the world of advertising, art directors and copywriters are notorious for their overflowing imaginations. But this creative *hubris is* strongly constrained by the advertiser's expectations: his goal is for his ad to "work", i.e., for his message to be remembered. Is this really the case? Brad J. Bushman and Angelica M. Bonacci (University of Iowa, U.S.A.) posed the question of the relationship between sex, violence and ad recall. Their study is limited to TV ads, which are the most watched, the most influential and, for that reason, the most expensive.

Bushman and Bonacci's study concerns not the ads themselves, but the TV programs in which these ad pages are inserted. They divided 328 adults (165 men, 163 women), aged 18 to 54, into three groups, each watching a different cathode-ray program: one with violent episodes, another with sexually explicit (erotic) episodes, a third being neutral. Each program lasted forty-five minutes, and was interspersed with nine identical commercials. After viewing the program, Bushman and Bonacci tested direct brand recall, recognition of brands seen (recall with suggestion) and delayed recall (after twenty-four hours).

The result of the study: advertisements inserted into violent or sexual programs have the worst recognition and memorization scores. This is true for both men and women, at all ages in the sample. The memorization score did not vary significantly according to whether viewers liked or disliked the program content (i.e. violence or eroticism).

The explanation proposed by Bushman and Bonacci is quite simple: the human brain's capacity for concentration and memory is limited. Yet this same brain is programmed to be attentive to stimuli of violence and sexuality, which obviously represent two important issues in human evolution. Moreover, the phenomenon of cognitive neo-association means that a violent or sexual stimulus tends to bring back to the surface in the viewer's brain personal memories involving these two registers. All the more reason to reduce the space available for advertising.

Contrary to what one might think after a quick read, the conclusions of this experiment by Bushman and Bonacci are rather positive for porno chic and, more generally, for the use of erotic content in advertising. For the effect of a sexually suggestive ad in the middle of a neutral TV program is likely to be maximal in terms of brand recall. Of course, advertisers are then confronted with other limits, notably the coherence of form and content. Leaving aside any ethical or aesthetic discussions, the display of a four-legged femme fatale wearing a dog collar can at best be understood as advertising perfume, pantyhose or any accessory involved in the game of desire and seduction. It's a bit more difficult for a brand of frozen food or washing powder…

Reference

B. J. Bushman and A. M. Bonacci (2002), "Violence and sex impair memory for television ads", *Journal of Applied Psychology*, 87, 557-564.

The Pain of puberty

Evolution of the age of puberty

Pedophilia is undoubtedly one of the most disapproved of crimes in Western public opinion today. The precise legal definition of paedophilia is not very clear, and can vary from one era or country to another. In French law, for example, sexual majority begins at the age of 15, but "minorité renforcée" protects children under the age of 13, by increasing penalties. Common sense generally distinguishes between childhood, adolescence and adulthood. A question implicitly raised by paedophilia is the limit of puberty, seen from the biological as well as the psychological point of view.

In a recent review, Peter D. Gluckman and Mark A. Hanson examine the evolution of puberty in the human species. Puberty is a complex phenomenon, manifested in humans by changes in the primary and secondary sexual characteristics of both sexes (genitalia, breasts, hair, voice). These physiological changes are accompanied by numerous psychological modifications. In the mammalian animal kingdom, puberty signals the onset of reproductive age.

160

In girls, the age of menarche varies. Several studies have shown that there is a genetic clock for this phenomenon, and perceptible differences between individuals or groups. But genes don't tell the whole story. Numerous studies have shown that lifestyle influences the expression of these genes: prenatal and postnatal stress, nutrition or endocrine disruptors can all affect the onset of menarche. This phenomenon is known as "developmental plasticity". It's not hard to explain: if evolution had selected a strict determinism of genes on the development of organisms, the slightest change in environment would have been fatal to entire populations. The fact that genetic (and in this case hormonal) signals are sensitive to environmental stimuli contributes to the adaptability of organisms.

What does this have to do with puberty? Its age has varied over the course of human evolution. Research into the earliest Homo sapiens of the Paleolithic period, including child skeletons, as well as contemporary hunter-gatherer populations whose lifestyle most closely resembles this, shows that the age of first menstruation was probably around 7 to 13 years, with reproductive capacity setting in around 9 to 14 years. On average, most girls were therefore fertile by the age of 10-12. Contrary to what we might think, the Neolithic period created unfavorable conditions that tended to delay puberty by several years. The increase in population density resulting from sedentarization, and the growth in trade, favoured the development of infectious diseases, which tend to delay development when they strike children. Food resources, now dependent on crops and livestock, have become more uncertain and irregular than those of hunting and gathering: many generations have experienced famines, and these also tend to delay the age of puberty (when they strike either the pregnant mother or the child after birth).

In terms of the reproductive age of young girls, our era is tending to return to... the Paleolithic. Living conditions have been steadily improving in developed societies for the past one hundred and fifty years, certain infectious childhood diseases are on the decline, and hygiene and nutrition have never been so favorable. As a result, the age of puberty has been falling steadily for four generations. Once again, children reach sexual maturity at around 10-11 years of age. The problem is that, at the same time, our industrialized societies have pushed back the age of marriage, with the symbolic status of man and woman considerably removed from actual reproductive capacity. As M. Hanson and P. Gluckman point out, "for the first time in the history of our species, biological maturation largely precedes psychosocial maturation".

The consequences of this growing discrepancy are, of course, numerous. From a medical point of view, we need to be cautious when diagnosing a child as having "precocious puberty", as this notion is obviously quite relative, and the appearance of the first menstrual period at around 7-8 years of age is not necessarily indicative of a hormonal imbalance. From a psychological and social point of view, we are and will increasingly be faced with the difficult task of reconciling the late preservation of a child's symbolic status with the gradual advancement of the reproductive period. Biology and society are evolving together, but not at the same pace.

Reference

P. D. Gluckman and M. A. Hanson (2006), "Changing times. The evolution of puberty", *Molecular and Cellular Endocrinology*, 254-255, 26-31.

Sex, Lies and Polls

Reliability of surveys on the number of sexual partners

Since the 1950s, major surveys have been conducted into the sex lives of our contemporaries. Some have led to famous publications (Hite, Kinsey, Masters & Johnson). Others are more modest epidemiological surveys, designed to model the transmission of sexually transmitted diseases. The results of these surveys generally give fairly accurate portraits of men's and women's sexual behavior. For example, when we ask about the number of partners in the past year, the frequency and average duration of sexual acts, and the acceptance of anal or oral sex, we obtain consistent responses across the samples.

But there is one problem area: the total number of sexual partners over the course of a lifetime. In all surveys, men report more partners than women - quite typically, responses range from 5 to 9 male partners and 8 to 14 female partners in people aged 40 and over. But it doesn't add up. The mathematical problem is quite simple: in quantitative surveys of heterosexual behavior, it is statistically impossible for the average number of partners to differ between the sexes. The dispersion of the result within each sex can certainly be different - that is, for example, a greater or lesser proportion in each sex of individuals with a very small or very large number of partners. But whatever this dispersion within the female and male populations, the average should be the same. But it isn't.

One explanation sometimes put forward for this statistical anomaly is poor survey sampling. Prostitutes, for example, have a very high number of sexual encounters, and their non-presence in the sample can lower the female average. But the inequality remains when subjects are asked not to include sex with prostitutes. Another explanation concerns partner recall: the men questioned would be inclined to give fairly approximate (and exaggerated) estimates quickly, whereas the women would tend to count each partner's recollections accurately. But this does not explain all the discrepancy between the two averages.

Let's face it: when it comes to sexuality, as in politics, respondents don't always tell pollsters the truth. Yes, but who's lying? Generally speaking, it's the men who are suspected of generously increasing their actual number of sexual conquests. To find out for sure, Michele G. Alexander and Teri D. Fisher (Universities of Ohio and Maine) asked 200 students aged 18 to 25 to fill in a questionnaire, under rather unusual conditions. The first group completed an anonymous questionnaire; the second group completed the same questionnaire, which could be read by the examiner; the third group answered the same questions... with a lie detector.

Result: whatever the method, the men's results hardly varied, ranging between 3.7 and 4.0 partners. The results for women were very different. Those who filled in their answers anonymously confessed to an average of 3.4 partners. Those whose answers were read by the examiners averaged just 2.6. And this figure climbed to... 4.4 when the students feared the polygraph verdict!

So it's women who tend to downplay their actual number of sexual partners in behavioral surveys. "We live in a culture that really expects a different attitude from each sex," stresses T. D. Fisher. In other words, the cliché is still alive and well that a man with many conquests is a seducer or a charmer, a woman in the same situation a nymphomaniac or a whore. Sex is said to be liberated, but mentalities aren't really.

Reference

M. G. Alexander and T. D. Fisher (2003), "Truth and conse-quences. Using the bogus pipeline to examine sex diffe-rences in self-reported sexuality", *Journal of Sex Research*, 40, 27-35.

Size Matters After All

The evolution of the male sex

Evolution has endowed male Homo sapiens with two beautiful organs: a large brain and a large penis. The male sex has an average length of between 127 and 178 mm when erect, and an average circumference of 24.5 mm. These dimensions are twice those of our closest cousin, the chimpanzee, and five times those of the gorilla, a little further down the primate family tree. The terminal bulge of the acorn is also unique.

Curiously, there are very few studies on women's preferences when it comes to their partners' sex size. The classic analyses by Masters and Johnson show a small minority who appreciate beautiful organs, and a majority who are indifferent. A 2003 survey by David A. Frederick (University of California, Los Angeles) of 50,000 adults aged 33-36 concluded that 85% of women are satisfied with the size of their partner's member. Russell Eisenman (Texas Pan American University, Edinburgh) surveyed 50 sexually active female students, asking them whether they attributed more importance to the length or thickness of their partners' penises. None of them answered that the question was indifferent. Of these students, 45 favored thickness over length, while 5 made the opposite choice. To explain this clear preference, the researcher hypothesizes that a wider penis enhances clitoral stimulation during intercourse.

It seems that men are more sensitive to penis size than women. D. A. Frederick's survey shows, for example, that 45% of males would prefer to have a larger penis, and that a majority tend to underestimate their size compared to the actual population average. This recurrent anxiety about sex size may, of course, have cultural origins, such as the widespread production of pornography in which male actors are particularly well endowed. But the long-standing and widespread association between the strength of the phallus and the representation of power suggests that the issue is less trivial than it might seem. Incidentally, a study carried out by Anthony F. Bogaert and Scott Hershberger on 5,122 men, including 935 homosexuals, showed that the average penis size of homosexuals was larger than that of heterosexuals.

If women really are insensitive to penis size, the very marked increase in penis size over the course of human evolution poses a problem. In fact, the sexual choices of females often determine the primary and secondary sexual characteristics of the males of their species: in the case of the penis, this rule should hold true. However, women seem to be rather indifferent. Another avenue of research for understanding the appearance of a sexual trait comes from competition between males. In 2004, Gordon G. Gallup and Rebecca L. Burch (New York University) put forward an interesting hypothesis: the human penis is configured to extract the sperm residues of potential competitors from a woman's vaginal canal.

And thus maximize the probability that the last ejaculate will be the right one (in reproductive terms, that is). Gallup and Burch base their hypothesis on MRI analyses of copulation, on reproductions of the act using artificial genitalia, and on the fact that couples frequently report more vigorous penetration in situations of potential infidelity (jealousy, separation, etc.). To which must be added, of course, the basic presupposition that a woman's copulation with different partners in a short space of time has been quite frequent over the last three million years, so that larger penises really have been at an advantage through natural selection. If we assume that pre-human and human populations were sometimes reduced to very small dimensions, the scenario is conceivable: an advantage could then rapidly gain the upper hand in this founding group, and then spread to its descendants.

Would our ancestors have happily practiced swinging and sexual pan-mixing, as in the utopias of Charles Fourier's *New World of Love?* The question remains open.

References

A. F. Bogaert and S. Hershberger (1999), "The relation between sexual orientation and penile size", *Archives of Sexual Behavior*, 28, 213-221.

R. Eisenman (2001), "Penis size. Survey of female perceptions of sexual satisfaction", *BMC Women's Health*, Online publication, June 8, 2001.

G. G. Gallup and R. L. Burch (2004), "Semen displacement as a sperm competition strategy in humans", *Evolutionary Psychology*, 2, 12-23.

The Hidden Advantages of Porn

Pornography and sperm quality

It's well known that men are far more interested in pornography than women. This taste for X is usually linked to the evolutionary sexual strategy of males, based more on the quantity of available partners than on the quality of lasting relationships. With millions of spermatozoa available at any one time, rather than a single egg every month, men are more inclined to have adventures for a day, or even an hour, if possible with different partners. And X, with its miraculous succession of copulation scenes between individuals who didn't know each other a quarter of an hour before, would satisfy this inclination. A recent study, however, suggests that men have at least one other reason to enjoy pornographic material: to maintain the quality of their sperm.

Leigh Simmons works in the Department of Evolutionary Biology at the University of Western Australia. With his assistant Sarah Kilgallon, the researcher looked at the effects of pornography on male sperm quality. Fifty-two heterosexual volunteers, aged between 18 and 35, were shown two explicit photographs one day apart. The first showed three women, the second one a woman and two men. These volunteers were asked to masturbate after the session, and the researchers then analyzed the number of sperm per milliliter of ejaculate, as well as their motility, i.e. their ability to move rapidly. Motility, which determines the ability to reach the oocyte for fertilization, is an important factor in male fertility. The 52 volunteers were also asked to complete a lifestyle questionnaire. And the size of their testicles was carefully measured.

Result: seeing a woman having sex with other men rather than other women improved sperm count ($76.64 \pm 1.26 \times 10^6$/ml vs. $61.35 \pm 1.27 \times 106$/ml) and the percentage of sperm with good motility ($52.1 \pm 7.3\%$ vs. $49.3 \pm 8.0\%$). Individuals who considered the photograph to be particularly explicit (and therefore unaccustomed to this kind of spectacle) had much better motility scores on average than the more blasé (58.7 vs. 38.0%). The novelty effect therefore plays a role in ejaculatory prowess. Other lifestyle factors showed a statistically significant association with sperm quality: drinking coffee in the preceding hours, having a partner and being sexually active (which would increase sperm count and motility); drinking alcohol, smoking, carrying your cell phone in your pocket or on your belt (which would decrease them).

How can we explain this result? By the eternal competition between males for access to females, which does not spare the human race. "Males ejaculate more sperm, or better quality sperm, when the risk of competition with other sperm is higher," summarizes Prof. Simmons. The mere sight of a woman already occupied by two competitors is apparently enough to set off an alarm signal indicating the imminence of a sexual challenge. A previous study of pornographic literature and the preferences of its male consumers showed that, among "threesomes", men tend to prefer two men and one woman to one man and two women (Pound, 2002). For consolation, or dismay, it's worth noting that the man is far from an isolated case. Birds shown a video of their nest being approached by other males are also breaking ejaculate records (Zbinden, 2004). The Homo sapiens male has inherited a long history as a competitor. For the females who have to put up with him - and, in this case, his X-rated films and websites - we can only suggest patience and understanding.

References

S. J. Kilgallon and L. W. Simmons (2005), "Image content influences men's semen quality", *Biology Letters*, 1, 253-255.

N. Pound (2002), "Male interest in visual cues of sperm competition risk", *Evolution and Human Behavior*, 23, 443-466.

M. Zbinden *et al.* (2004), "Body size of virtual rivals affects ejaculate size in sticklebacks", *Behavioral Ecology*, 15, 137-140.

Are Cuckolds Weird?

Facial asymmetry and jealousy

Pantalon, the jealous, possessive old man in commedia dell'arte who is regularly cuckolded by his young wife, is often depicted hunched over, hook-nosed and ungainly through and through. This literary figure could be of interest to specialists in human behavior in more ways than one.

Researchers have long been interested in the symmetry of bodies and faces. Symmetry is known to be positively correlated with health, fertility, intelligence and attractiveness. William Brown and Chris Moore from the University of Halifax (Canada) deduced that people with asymmetrical features must be more jealous than average: "If jealousy is a way of keeping your partner, then the individuals who are most likely to be cheated on are the ones who will be the most jealous. Similarly, those with the fewest desirable traits are more likely to have their partner go elsewhere."

To confirm or refute this hypothesis, the scientists gathered 25 men and 25 women, with an average age of 20.29, and measured their symmetry rate. Called FA, for *fluctuating asymmetry*, this measure was invented in 1962 by Van Valen. It quantifies small variations from perfect bilateral symmetry of morphological features. Here, the FA of the volunteers was calculated from the measurement, accurate to 0.01 mm, and comparison of 11 bilateral morphological features such as the length and width of feet, ears, hips, knees and fingers. Volunteers were then asked to complete two questionnaires. The first, the Interpersonal Jealousy Scale, was a 28-item questionnaire assessing their propensity to be jealous, in the context of marriage and love. A second questionnaire assessed jealousy in a non-sexual context. It consisted of two entries: "Someone gets the promotion that was intended for you" and "Someone takes away the honors or benefits of something you've accomplished". These situations were to be rated on a 9-point scale, from "not very jealous" to "very jealous".

The results showed a correlation between trait asymmetry and sexual jealousy in both sexes. On the other hand, there was no correlation between trait asymmetry and jealousy in non-sexual situations, as described in the second questionnaire. Jealousy is a rather costly practice from an evolutionary point of view, as it requires time and energy, and sometimes leads to violence and death. Jealousy would be a behavior that indicates not only the actual propensity to be deceived according to circumstances, but also the value of the jealous partner in the midst of the army of rivals. A poor potential for symmetry at the outset would thus translate into a high potential for jealousy at the end.

Reference

W. M. Brown and C. Moore (2003), "Fluctuating asymmetry and romantic jealousy", *Evolution and Human Behavior*, 24, 113-117.

DIVORCE WAS PREDICTABLE

Differential equations of conjugal relationships

John Gottman's ambition is simple: "To become like the inventor of Velcro - nobody remembers his name, yet everyone uses it." Since 1979, this psychologist from the University of Washington has been conducting projects at his Seattle family research laboratory (dubbed the "Love Lab") aimed at the scientific study of marital relationships. His work involves observing couples in conversation, taking physiological and psychological measurements, and then creating mathematical models to integrate the correlations between all these elements and make some predictions about couples' lives.

Gottman trained as a mathematician. He prepared his doctorate at MIT, which he abandoned, according to legend, because he found his psychologist roommate's books more interesting than his own. Nevertheless, the young researcher would carry the weight of his initial training with him all his life: reality only makes sense if it can be translated into mathematical terms. Ironically, or as fate would have it, Gottman was going through a difficult period in his marriage - his wife, who was pregnant, asked him to take a break from his research to devote himself to their budding family life. Despite the quarrels, Gottman's marriage survived (his wife Julie Schwartz Gottman is now one of his closest collaborators).

Around this time, he came across a book by James Murray entitled *Mathematical Biology*. In it, Murray proposes to apply a system of non-linear equations to understand the complex mechanisms of dynamic systems such as the growth of brain tumors. No sooner had he finished reading it than Gottman let out his eureka! The universality that had been missing from his research was in his hands, and the program was set: "We are as social as bees. Von Frisch discovered the language of bees by going into the hives and watching them dance. Now it's up to us to understand human dance." So Gottman invites Murray, who also teaches at Seattle University, to talk to him about his fusion project: "At the beginning of the meal," Murray explains, "I thought his idea of involving mathematics in his research on marriage was completely ridiculous. But by the end of the lunch, when I grasped what he had in mind, I was simply transfixed."

At the end of this collaboration, the two men seem to have finally found the equation for the perfect marriage. They have devised a model that reliably predicts a couple's risk of divorce. Their technique, tested over the last ten years on several hundred couples, predicts, in 94% of cases, whether the couple will divorce within five years, or whether they are built to last. Gottman and Murray took as their raw material fifteen minutes of video recordings of hundreds of couples discussing a contentious issue. They awarded one point for each positive interaction between the

Odds and Ends

man and the woman, and withdrew one point for each negative interaction. They also analyzed and integrated into their model the facial expressions and heartbeats of both people (above one hundred beats per minute, the body begins to produce adrenaline, making the mind less receptive to the other's arguments). The result was quantified as a ratio between positive and negative interactions. "The magic ratio is 5 (positive) to 1 (negative)," explained the researchers, for whom all couples with a ratio of less than 5 to 1 are at risk.

When a good equation is better than seven years' thought...

Reference

J. M. Gottman and J. Murray (2005), *The Mathematics of Marriage. Dynamic Nonlinear Models*, Cambridge (MA), Bradford Books.

FEWER AND FEWER CHILDREN?

Human reproductive optimum

The idea that women's fertility remains intact until the age of 30 or 40 is certainly reassuring for those who choose to work and delay their first pregnancy. But from an evolutionary point of view, it makes little sense. For most of human history, with life expectancy quite low by modern standards, we can predict that reproduction has been optimized for the years immediately following puberty.

According to an international team led by David B. Dunson, the decline in female fertility begins as early as age 20, and not at age 30 as previously thought. His team drew on the results of a previous study involving 782 healthy couples (349 with at least one pregnancy). The women were divided into three age groups: 19-26, 27-29 and 30-34. All these couples were using natural contraception. The scientists collected information on a total of 5,860 menstrual cycles. The date of ovulation, determined from a basal body temperature reading, enabled a fertility window of six days to be drawn, roughly stable regardless of the woman's age. As a result, 433 pregnancies were detected out of 2,539 unprotected cycles. What changes is the probability of becoming pregnant during this period, which is halved between the 19-26 and 30-34 age groups. In addition, women show a very high degree of variability in fertility, without the cause being identified - probably a combination of genetic, epidemiological and environmental factors.

Will women who delay pregnancy for career reasons find their lineage excluded from the gene pool in the long term? To answer this question, Bobbi Low and colleagues (Institute for Social Research, University of Michigan) have developed a complex computer simulation, involving 9 socio-economic levels and over 900 parameters on living conditions and reproductive choices. The basic problem is as follows: in most species and environments, lineages with fewer offspring on average than others almost always end up being excluded, and the best way to prevail is to have children as early in life as possible; but in the human species, whose environment is highly competitive from a cognitive point of view, numerically fewer offspring can be attractive if they receive a strong parental investment, which will translate into better health, abundant resources and greater ease of starting a couple. Running their model over 220 years (for a simulated generation of 5 years, i.e. 44 generations), Bobbi Low found that wealthy, healthy women giving birth late (after the age of 35) drop from 11% to 5% of the population. The poorest suffer a similar fate. The prize goes to middle-class women (33% to 60%). Regardless of economic status, a first child in one's early twenties is part of the "winning" strategy. Low, who herself gave birth to her first child in her mid-thirties, nevertheless points out that most modern women don't really have the long-term evolutionary success of their reproductive strategy in mind!

Contrary to what you might think, men are not spared this threat of reproductive decline either, even though they ignore the menopause and produce sperm continuously. In fact, their fertility declines considerably from the age of 35 onwards. Dunson's study showed a negative correlation between a man's age and the risk of pregnancy: a couple in which both members are 35 has a 0.29 probability of pregnancy in unprotected intercourse, compared with only 0.18 when the man is 5 years older. Like women, but to a lesser extent, men are subject to an internal biological clock that regulates their procreative life. According to another study conducted by Narendra Singh on 60 men aged between 22 and 60, sperm motility is reduced and the nuclear DNA of gametes is more frequently damaged after the age of 35. In addition to increasing reproductive difficulties, this can lead to a rise in childhood pathologies, including malformations and early cancers.

The most beautiful age of life can therefore be interpreted in two ways, depending on whether we're talking about the life of the adult or that of the unborn child. The age of 20 seems to be the best for enjoying life and giving life. But these realities have become contradictory for many couples in industrialized societies.

References

B. Colombo and G. Masarotto (2000), "Daily fecundability. First results from a new data base", *Demographic Research*, 3, 39.

B. S. Low (2000), "Sex, wealth, and fertility. Old rules, new environments", *in* L. Cronk (ed.), *Adaptation and Human Behavior. An Anthropological Perspective*, New York, Aldine de Gruyter.

D. B. Dunson *et al* (2002), "Changes with age in the level and duration of fertility in the menstrual cycle", *Human Reproduction*, 17, 1399-1403.

N. P. Singh *et al* (2003), "Effects of age on DNA double-strand breaks and apoptosis in human sperm", *Fertility and Sterility*, 80, 1420-1430.

Does the G-spot Exist?

Anatomy of vaginal pleasure

Few subjects have generated as much ink as the G-spot. The term refers to an area of the vagina capable of giving a woman an intense orgasm, sometimes accompanied by ejaculation.

A little history first. In 1950, German gynecologist Ernest Gräfenberg published his first observations. He reported that some of his patients derived a singular pleasure from inserting objects (notably hat needles!) into the urethra. Gräfenberg is content with this observation and does not speak of a specific erogenous or orgasmic zone. He also hypothesizes that this stimulation may be accompanied by the secretion of a liquid other than urine.

Gräfenberg's work was forgotten for three decades. At the time, the major reports on sexuality (Kinsey, Hite, Masters and Johnson) concluded that women's pleasure was essentially clitoral, not vaginal. This conclusion was vigorously supported by the feminist movement, anxious to dissociate the female orgasm from the male-dependent coitus so detested. The subject is as much medical as it is ideological. However, Gräfenberg's orgasmic zone came back into fashion in the early 1980s, under the name of the "G-spot". It enjoyed immense popularity, bolstered by this mysterious name and the idea that any woman could somehow become a "sex beast" if she discovered her G-spot.

Anatomically speaking, there are two candidate areas for the G-spot. The first is formed by the Skene glands, sometimes incorrectly referred to as the "female prostate". This is a network of glands located at the interface of the urethra and vagina, but is not present in all women. This would explain why the G-spot (and vaginal orgasm in general) is not universally felt. Another candidate zone is the erectile tissue of the vagina, whose existence has been demonstrated by ultrasound, but whose location does not correspond exactly to Gräfenberg's observations on the erogenous zone. The "real" G-spot is supposed to be located 4-5 cm from the vulval orifice, on the anterior wall of the vagina.

Data on female ejaculation from the urethra or its periphery are even rarer. There are many possible secretions during a sexual act: urine, leucorrhoea, vaginal transudate, excretions from the Skene or Bartholin glands. The problem is that no precise mechanism has yet been identified for ejaculation itself, described by some as the sustained, jerky propulsion of a liquid out of the vulva.

What about women's testimonials? An initial large-scale questionnaire survey of 2,350 women (55% of respondents), all working in the health sector and with varying degrees of knowledge of anatomy, concluded that two-thirds were able to experience vaginal pleasure, and had at least one pleasure zone. Among those who claimed to have identified their G-spot, 82%

reported ejaculation during orgasm. These sizeable figures have not, however, been replicated in all subsequent studies.

In the early 2000s, Terence M. Hines reviewed the entire scientific literature on the G-spot and provocatively concluded that it was a "modern gynecological myth". However, the researcher drew four critical retorts from his colleagues, who believed that the G-spot existed in some of their patients. The controversy is still raging, and debates continue in the scientific community.

So, does the G-spot exist? At present, we can't give a definitive answer to this question. Three provisional conclusions can be drawn: vaginal orgasm is a reality for some women; this orgasm can be obtained by stimulating certain zones located between the vagina and the urethra; if the G-spot exists, it's highly likely that not all women have it, and it's possible that the erogenous/orgasmic zone varies according to anatomy. Here, as elsewhere, there are the lucky few and the rest.

References

C. A. Darling *et al.* (1990), "Female ejaculation. Perceived origins, the Grafenberg spot/area, and sexual responsiveness", *Archives of Sexual Behavior*, 19, 29-47.

T. M. Hines (2001), "The G-spot. A modern gynecologic myth", *American Journal of Obstetrics and Gynecology*, 185, 359-362.

Epilogue:
A Brief History of Sex

Nature loves sex

There's no doubt about it, nature loves sex: around 95% of known plant and animal species are sexual. Yet a number of them reproduce perfectly without sex, either by fission (cloning, chosen by single-celled animals) or by parthenogenesis. The method is economical, as it saves the species concerned from having to produce two types of reproductive cells (gametes), from having to invent all the strange machinery of sexual attractors to stimulate desire, and from wasting enormous amounts of energy on rites of seduction and copulation exercises. Parthenogenesis is just as effective: in ten generations, it has been calculated that a "typical" asexual species produces a thousand times more offspring than a sexual species. Cloning and parthenogenesis are also fairly reliable methods, since bacteria have been reproducing in this way since the origins of life.

So why has evolution invented and above all preserved sexual reproduction, using male and female cells? Because, although more complicated at first glance, it offers several selective advantages.

Asexual reproduction produces clones: apart from mutations, children are perfectly similar to their parents. The invention of sex has changed all this: parents each give only 50% of their genome (randomly selected during meiosis) to their children. The result is greater diversity between the individuals of the species. This diversity is advantageous in at least three situations: genetic mutations, ecological adaptation and parasite resistance.

Genetic mutations, which result, for example, from DNA copying errors, are most often deleterious to the individual who carries them. Asexual reproduction tends to accumulate them rapidly, since mutated genes are transmitted identically from generation to generation. In sexual reproduction, the chances of transmitting mutations are minimized, since the mutated gene from the father must be inherited at the same time as that from the mother, at the end of the great lottery of genetic recombi-nation. Sexual reproduction thus results in individuals carrying mutations in the heterozygous state (only one copy out of two): the bad ones stabilize or are gradually eliminated from the gene pool; the good ones enable adaptation to environmental changes.

This ecological adaptation is the second advantage of sex. When the environment changes, asexual reproduction offers little flexibility, with all offspring identical to their parents except for a few mutations. Sex, on the other hand, produces greater variability: individuals unsuited to change disappear, while others survive. Some species strangely combine the advantages of both modes of reproduction. This is the case of aphids, for example. When resources are abundant, aphids reproduce by parthenogenesis;

but as soon as their environment becomes impoverished, they switch to sexual reproduction, which diversifies the offspring.

The third advantage of sexual reproduction is resistance to parasites. Parasites - viruses, bacteria, worms, etc. - co-evolve with their hosts, constantly adapting to one another. In this game, parasites are champions because of the frequency of their mutations. However, animals resulting from fission or parthenogenesis don't have much to answer for in this respect: their offspring are adapted to the same parasites as their parents. If a parasite evolves into a slightly more greedy or virulent form, dangerous for its host, the whole line is threatened. Sexual reproduction, on the other hand, enables the development of a wide range of anti-parasite defenses.

MAKING WAR, MAKING LOVE

A 1970s adage suggested making love rather than war. Yet the two activities are not always so far apart in the history of life.

For proof of this, we need look no further than atypical species such as praying mantises or tarantulas, where the female willingly devours the male after mating. By increasing the diversity of individuals within the same species, sexual reproduction provokes numerous potential conflicts between these individuals: those who do not find their alter ego in the other sex perish without leaving any descendants. To transmit its genes, not only does it need to find one or more partners, it also needs to know how to choose the right one or ones. A vast program. Darwin called this permanent pressure exerted by evolution "sexual selection". It's the reason why deer grow huge antlers, why bombyxes produce powerful pheromones, why albatrosses dance wildly during mating season, and why some men work out and some women have plastic surgery!

In addition to their primary sexual characteristics (genitalia and physiological differences related to reproduction), both animals and humans develop secondary sexual characteristics: these do not contribute directly to sexuality or fertility, but play a role in mate selection. There is therefore competition within each sex to choose the best partner or offer the best assets. But there is also competition between the sexes, who do not have the same reproductive strategies. To wage war, you don't need to know how to make love. But to make love, it's better to know how to make war!

Males and females therefore differ in their sexual behavior. This difference is inscribed in the very mechanisms of sexuality and reproduction. While the pleasure of sex is important to us, and relatively independent of kinship, it's important to remember that evolution doesn't reason the way we do: it's the quality and quantity of offspring that interest it.

In 1966, George C. William pointed out: "The essential role of a male mammal may end with copulation, which requires a negligible expenditure of energy and material on his part, and only a momentary loss of attention as regards his safety and well-being. The situation is very different for the female, for whom copulation can mean a commitment to a prolonged load, in the mechanical and physical sense, with the attendant stress and dangers."

Based on this initial intuition, Robert Trivers founded the theory of parental investment in 1972. From a Darwinian point of view, success in copulation does not mean success in reproduction: not only must the male ensure that the female receives his sperm and not those of a competitor, but the resulting offspring must also survive. An individual's reproductive success is therefore always the combination of two distinct processes: partner conquest (time and energy spent on seduction) and parental investment (time and energy spent on caring for offspring).

This parental investment is of course influenced by the reproductive capacities of each sex. The sex with the highest reproductive potential will tend to favor the search for the greatest number of partners, while the other will be inclined to increase parental investment. This pattern is all the more true when the care of both parents is not necessary for the survival of the children.

Gender asymmetry begins even before procreation, with the formation of reproductive cells. The first difference between the female and the male lies in the energy and time they invest in developing their gamete. In the human species, as in most mammals, the ovum is large and rare; the spermatozoon tiny and abundant.

For an equivalent expenditure of nutrients and energy, the female produces one ovum per month, the male several million spermatozoa per day. Moreover, internal gestation and lactation in mammals require sacrifices from the female that the male is unaware of. At a disadvantage, the female has every interest in being selective in her choice of partner: either the best match to produce beautiful children, or the best match to make a good parent. And if possible, both.

Epilogue: A Brief History of Sex

A female's selectivity thus reinforces the competition between her suitors. In her quest for the ideal male partner, the beauty of an ornament, the quality of a song, the complexity of a courtship ritual, the vigor of a fight are good qualitative indicators: only physically and genetically well-endowed males can take on the effort required to develop these secondary sexual traits. For this reason, the sex with the greatest internal competition (usually the male) is also the one with the most pronounced individual differences.

While these two fundamental tendencies are found in all sexual reproduction, they naturally vary from species to species. Robert Trivers also predicted that parental investment would be reversible according to gender role. And so it is. In the European plover and the red-necked phalarope, for example, it is the fathers who build the nest, incubate the eggs and feed the young after birth. Logically, it is the females of these two species who compete to woo the males.

These differences explain how the sexes approach mating and parental care. It has been shown that in 95% of known mammalian species, females are responsible for parental care. Interestingly, primates (and most carnivorous species) stand out for their more pronounced paternal care, present in 30 to 40% of species (including man, of course).

A visit to our close primate cousins allows us to observe this competition between males and females.

In non-monogamous species (chimpanzees, bonobos, macaques, mandrills, baboons...), competition between males for group dominance and access to females is a permanent feature, whether this competition concerns individuals or coalitions of individuals. Failing to block access to resources, dominant males aim for social and sexual control of other group members, whatever their sex, with a more severe focus on females when they are in the receptive, i.e. fertile, period. In this case, dominance is often correlated with male hormone levels (testosterone), resulting in significant dimorphism between the sexes.

Genetic paternity tests carried out by researchers on monkeys have shown that this strategy pays off. An eleven-year study on baboons, for example, concluded that the alpha (dominant) male, called Radi, was indeed the father of 81% of the offspring born during his four-year reign. Before and after his domination of the group and territory, Radi was involved in only one-fifth of all births...

Social dominance is not the only strategy observed in primate species. Lower-ranking males can take advantage of the choice of females either to deceive the dominant or to form longer-lasting monogamous unions. Both sexes benefit. In this way, the male avoids the risk of non-descendence posed by the domination of the alpha individual. The female, by maintaining a longer-lasting relationship with a male, minimizes physical risks during periods of social conflict and increases parental investment in her offspring.

The choice of females (the second dimension of sexual selection after competition between males) also plays an important role in primates. As a general rule, females choose to maintain friendly (and amorous) relationships with males higher up the hierarchy. Conversely, dominant males are highly indiscriminate in their choice of mates, seeking out quantity above all else. In sixteen primate species, there is also female-female competition, between individuals or coalitions. The object of such aggression, which is always less violent than in males, may be the defense of resources, the protection of children, or the maintenance of social hierarchy (i.e. restricting other females' access to the dominant male's circle).

Monogamous or polygamous

As the human species didn't appear out of nowhere, we can expect our sexual and marital regimes to bear the imprint of our origins.

For several centuries, the accounts of explorers and then the investigations of ethnologists have revealed the astonishing diversity of the human race in terms of marriage systems and sexual mores. The human species practices monogamy, polygyny (several women for one man) as well as polyandry (several men for one woman).

Polyandry is exceptional in the human species. It affects less than 1% of ethnic groups worldwide: Aleuts in Greenland, Nayar and Toda in India, Nyinba in Nepal and Tibet. This extremely rare family system in humans (as in other species) has developed under extreme ecological and economic conditions, when the presence of at least two men is necessary to ensure the family's subsistence.

The only polygynous unions in which one man is involved with several women are generally referred to as "polygamous".

Ethnological studies have counted over 950 cultures worldwide practicing polygamy. Three-quarters of all human societies recognize or even encourage polygamy, making it the most common form of sexual union in our species. Monogamy, however, dominates numerically, due to the demographic superiority of the cultures concerned. It is estimated that in monogamous societies, around 5% of births are the result of extramarital affairs.

Does human sexuality follow the general trend of other animal species? Yes, there are four main sexual regimes in nature. Promiscuity, widespread among mammals and insects, refers to the system where males and females mate without establishing any real associations. A sort of permanent orgy. Polygyny is also common in mammals, where the dominant male of the group surrounds himself with a harem that is sometimes egalitarian, sometimes hierarchical (with a high-ranking female). Monogamy is rare in mammals (5% of species), but very dominant in birds (over 80% of species), due to the immaturity of newborns and their high metabolic needs: a single-parent family would have little chance of survival.

Human sexuality, which is predominantly polygamous with a strong monogamous component, is therefore common to all mammals. Most anthropoid apes - gorillas, chimpanzees, baboons - are polygynous, with the exception of orangutans, whose males and females are solitary, and gibbons, which are monogamous.

In the evolutionary logic we adopt here, human polygamy can be explained by the biological characteristics of both sexes. The male, being of more powerful stature than the female, tends to provide for security and supply (especially of scarce resources

Epilogue: A Brief History of Sex

such as meat): he translates this commensality into sexuality. Moreover, males tend to invest more in mating competition than in parental care.

As for monogamy, its main advantage is to maximize parental investment (two adults to nurture and educate the couple's children): a useful provision for a species with high cognitive development like ours. Monogamy also ensures social peace by reducing competition between males in societies with roughly equal numbers of each sex. On the other hand, it accentuates competition between women - a trend reflected, for example, in the massive use of make-up and cosmetics designed to accentuate the image of beauty, health and youthfulness. Depending on how you look at it, each system has its virtue: in a polygamous system, almost every woman has the right to a man; in a monogamous system, almost every man has the right to a woman!

Stay-at-home dad and multiple lovers...

Other phenomena than the management of resources according to sexual dimorphism explain the variations in love and family relationships among Homo sapiens. In particular, there are certain secrets that women are very good at keeping.

In nature, sexuality is often simpler than in the human species. It is codified by fairly strict and repetitive mechanisms. The ratio of sexually active males to sexually active females at a given time and in a given area of the breeding territory is known as the "operational sex ratio" (ORS). In some species, the ORS is influenced by the receptivity of females, i.e. the ovulatory period when signs (turgidity, postures, pheromones) inviting copulation appear.

In humans, unlike many other species, female ovulation is not indicated to the male by external physiological changes (reddening of the vulva, for example), nor by perceptible chemical messages (pheromones). Certain signals are indeed perceived, as we have seen several times in this book, but unconsciously. So a man never knows precisely when a woman is likely to be impregnated. Especially as she tends to be sexually receptive and attractive throughout her menstrual cycle.

This dual characteristic - hidden ovulation and permanent receptivity - has undoubtedly played a significant role in the evolution of hominids. There are two opposing hypotheses: the stay-at-home dad or multiple lovers.

For biologists Richard Alexander and Katharine Noonan, discreet ovulation has favored monogamy: to ensure that he is indeed the father of his offspring, and to ward off potential competitors, the man has had to stay with his mate more often. A task made more pleasant by the fact that the woman is always sexually receptive. This is the stay-at-home dad hypothesis.

Primatologist Sarah Hrdy prefers the hypothesis of multiple lovers. We recently learned that, in addition to humans, many other species - lions, wild dogs, chimpanzees, gorillas, etc. - practice infanticide: when a male has successfully fought off a competitor and taken possession of his harem, it's not uncommon for him to kill all the newborns. In so doing, he simultaneously eliminates the last genetic vestiges of his predecessor and the mother's lactation, triggering a new ovulatory cycle.

According to S. Hrdy, the woman's hidden ovulation and permanent sexual receptivity enable her to sleep with several males without any of them being completely certain of her paternity. This doubt reduces the male's desire for infanticide. What's more, multiple copulations (common among our closest chimpanzee and bonobo cousins) encourage "sperm competition" and increase the probability of a female being impregnated by the best sire. In other words, in the course of human evolution, the woman has had all the Darwinian advantages to make her infidelity pay off: the resources and protection of the official father, the qualities of the biological father...

In fact, as physiologist Jared Diamond points out, the two theories don't necessarily cancel each other out. "In the common ancestors of humans, gorillas and chimpanzees, the females who best masked their ovulation and thus avoided infanticide had more offspring. When this trait became fixed, females were able to use it to attach themselves to a partner, so as to benefit permanently from his protection."

THE MOST BEAUTIFUL ORGAN OF SEX: OUR BRAIN!

Sexuality is a real puzzle for human beings. According to a recent hypothesis by Geoffrey Miller, psychologist and researcher at University College (London), this complexity may even be at the origin of our species' unique intellectual faculties.

Its point of departure is an enigma, the central enigma of our species: why did man become man so quickly, so obviously detached from other primates? More precisely, any satisfactory theory of the human mind inspired by biology and evolution must explain at least three problems.

First question: why are large, complex brains so rare in evolution? 99.5% of animals have brains smaller than that of the chimpanzee (500 g). Only the great apes, elephants and certain marine mammals rank higher on the encephalization scale. Evolution doesn't seem to appreciate consciousness or intelligence too much, as it endows most animals with a very low capacity in this area. Yet human experience bears witness to the adaptive advantages of intelligence. Let's not forget that the human brain is the most complex organ ever produced by evolution: on average, it weighs just 1,400 g, or 2% of our body mass, but consumes 20% of the body's energy resources. In the absence of precise uses, it's hard to imagine a favorable and lasting selection of these hundreds of billions of neurons...

Second question: why is there such a long time gap between the increase in the size of the human brain and its first concrete, i.e. technological, manifestations? Over a period of two million years, our brain tripled in volume without any significant change in stone size. For at least 150,000 years (and perhaps three times as long), there were anatomically modern humans, comparable to us, with no tangible (or abundant) traces of art, cities, technologies, burials, etc. Evolution had not been "the first" to develop. Evolution didn't "foresee" our 5,000 years of recent history when it forged an organ as energy-intensive as the brain over hundreds of thousands of years...

Third question: what might be the adaptive values of certain universal properties of the human mind, such as humor, story-telling, art, music, self-awareness, ideology, religion, morality, articulate language, song, poetry, etc.? Some of these "innovations" seem perfectly useless from an evolutionary point of view... yet their universality is obvious, suggesting that they are part of human nature. Hence biology. Hence evolution.

If we reason in evolutionary terms, we must try to find the adaptive function of these universal traits, bearing in mind that the "chance side effect" and "random emergent properties" hypotheses are not the most satisfactory. For G. Miller, sexual selection is the only correct answer to all three questions, explaining all three phenomena simultaneously. And for a very simple reason. Natural selection (competition for survival) is relatively slow and "stupid": it depends above all on inert factors (the environment, whose modification is often small on the life scale of a species) and chance factors (genetic mutations, ecological catastrophes). Conversely, sexual selection is rapid, reciprocal and "creative". As cognition develops (perception, learning, memory), the choice of mate becomes increasingly selective, precise and therefore directive. This is why secondary sexual traits can develop very quickly, being the object of directional pressure in every generation. It can produce the peacock's long tail... or a man's big brain. This "race forward" process of sexual selection is known as the "feedback loop". The more a trait is desired, the more it is selected; the more it is selected, the more it spreads through the population, and the less differential advantage it brings; desire then turns to a new trait, which is selected... and so on.

For the 200,000 pre-human and human generations that have preceded us since the age of the australopithecines Abel and Lucy, the first problem was to survive, in other words: to feed, to escape predators, conflicts and disease. But beyond simple survival, the second fundamental problem of the short Pleistocene existence was: how do I seduce the person I want to spend the night with or start a couple? All teenagers and young adults ask themselves this question very often today. There's no reason to think they weren't asking it yesterday...

From this point of view, a large number of features that we attribute globally to "culture" (an umbrella term that is ultimately rather vague) can be interpreted in the light of the sexual selection hypothesis: music and song expressing emotions and sensations in such a strange way, games and competitions enabling men to show off (and not endangering their lives like wars), adornments, attributes, ornaments, tattoos and scarification magnifying bodies, art with explicit sexual content (the callipygous Venuses) or with an implicit sexual function (valorizing the creator through his creativity), etc. The Darwinian revolution," notes Geoffrey Miller, "can only conquer the citadel of human nature by transforming itself into a sexual revolution, that is, by paying more attention to sexual choice as a driving force in the evolution of the mind.

References: a few basics to take you further

D. P. Barash and J. E. Lipton (2002), The Myth of Monogamy. Fidelity and Infidelity in Animals and People, New York, W. H. Freeman.

D. M. Buss (1995), The Evolution of Desire. Strategies of Human Mating, New York, Basic Books.

M. Daly and M. Wilson (1983), *Sex, Evolution, and Behavior,* Belmont (California), Wadsworth.

C. Darwin (1871, 1999), *La Filiation de l'homme et la sélection liée au sexe*, Paris, Syllepses.

J. M. Diamond (1998), *Why is Sex Fun? The Evolution of Human Sexuality*, Nairn, Ness, Theatrenutz Book Company.

A. Forsyth (1993), *A Natural History of Sex. The Ecology and Evolution of Eating Behavior*, Shelburne, Chapters Publishing.

D. C. Geary (2003), *Men, Women. The evolution of human sexual differences*, Brussels, De Boeck.

S. B. Hrdy (2001), *La Femme qui n'évoluait jamais*, Paris, Payot.

G. Miller (2001), *The Eating Mind. How Sexual Choice Shaped the Evolution of Human Nature*, London, Vintage.

M. Ridley (1994), *The Red Queen: Sex and the Evolution of Human Nature*, New York, Penguin Books.

R. Trivers (2002), *Natural Selection and Social Theory*, London, Oxford University Press.

G. C. Williams (1966), *Adaptation and Natural Selection*, Princeton (New Jersey), Princeton University Press.

Table of Contents

SECOND PART

Desire, Pleasure and Seventh Heaven

THIRD PART

The Brain in Love

PART FOUR

Hormones, Pheromones and other Odors

PART FIVE
Menstrual Cycle, Sexual Cycle

Best sellers Max Milo Editions

Hitler's banker, Jean-François Bouchard

Confessions of a forger, Éric Piedoie Le Tiec

The Koran and the flesh, Ludovic-Mohamed Zahed

Governing by fake news, Jacques Baud

Governing by chaos, Collectif

A political history of food, Paul Ariès

Mad in U.S.A.: The ravages of the "American model",
Michel Desmurget

Mondial soccer club geopolitics, Kévin Veyssière

Putin: Game master?, Jacques Braud

Treatise on the three impostors: Moses, Jesus, Muhammad,
The Spirit of Spinoza

TV Lobotomy, Michel Desmurget

Printed by Libri Plureos GmbH in Hamburg,
Germany